P9-CDF-101

"I challenge anyone to read this book without having a holiday in their heart. Hammett not only showcases how hope is the distinguishing mark of a vital church, but turns this book into a rope of hope to transform no-hope and low-hope living into high-hope communities of faith."

Leonard Sweet, Author, Professor
(Drew University, George Fox University)
Chief Contributor to sermons.com

"In *Recovering Hope for Your Church*, Eddie Hammett offers an excellent resource for congregational leaders seeking to help their church move into a healthy and vital future. Using the analogy of diagnosing and treating the human body, he presents treatment options based upon biblical examples, current change research, and his own extensive experience working with congregations. This book gives leaders tools for assessing a church's current condition, and its possibilities for innovation and spiritual transformation."

Peggy Hinds, Congregational and Leadership Coach
Educator and Mid-Council Leader, Presbyterian Church (USA)

"*Recovering Hope for Your Church* is practical, accessible, and saturated with wisdom. It will help you deal with congregational realities from church bullies to fear of change, from being over-programmed to thinking you're friendly when you're actually not, from refocusing your purpose to developing a healthy culture, and so much more. A gift for pastors and lay leaders alike from a wise and seasoned coach."

Brian McLaren, Author, Speaker, Activist

"Eddie Hammett knows congregational ministry. He begins this discussion with 'Why?' and leads us to 'How!' Eddie takes us on a fascinating journey from the 'institutional' church that is focused purely on itself through the Missional church to its next expression. The Incarnational Church is a transformed, redeemed body of Christ. Along the way, Eddie poses coaching questions that give readers opportunities to think, reflect, and act. This is pure Hammett at his best, insightful, informational, inspirational!"

Bo Prosser, Ministries Coordinator
Cooperative Baptist Fellowship

"In many ways the church of Jesus Christ is not healthy and it's losing hope. That's why Eddie Hammett's book is the right word at just the right time. Drawing upon his personal experience as well as expertise in congregational coaching, Eddie offers pastors and church leaders a way to rediscover hope and experience new energy for the future. Through his diagnosis of the times, as well as his coaching resources, pastors and church leaders will be able to embark on a journey of dreaming and discovery that will reenergize their passion for Christ as well as the Great Commission. If you feel your church is stuck, your next step needs to be to go and purchase this book. It will be your first huge step toward renewal."

Scott Wagoner, Pastoral Minister
Deep River Friends Meeting (Quaker)

"Facing a life-threatening health crisis creates an opportunity to discover the truths of recovering hope for congregations with uncertain futures. Eddie Hammett brings his years of congregational work and coaching experience to face his own uncertainty and in doing so discovers a way of transformation for churches struggling to stay alive in a context of change. Congregational coaching in *Recovering Hope* is the 'yes' to the question of how. Intentionality, truth telling, honest conversation, teachable moments, laughter, struggle, and hospitality are coached practices that create shared passion and move churches forward. When top-down hierarchies of power and pre-planned agendas are set aside, the Spirit finds welcome in this sacred space of being together. *Recovering Hope* shares stories of congregational transformation and provides the tools for churches and coaches to find the courage to let go of what threatens health and embrace that which brings new life."

Carol Morgan, Chaplain
North Carolina Department of Health and Human Services

"Eddie Hammett offers a pinpoint diagnosis of the challenges facing 21st-century churches in a changing culture. Framed through the lens of his health crisis, Hammett's thirty years of working, consulting, and coaching with ministry leaders provides a front row seat on the issues many churches face. His stories and insights, coupled with pertinent questions and assessment tools in each chapter, offer hopeful prescriptions for a coach approach process encouraging church leaders to embrace a Spirit-led future."

Greg Rogers, Pastor, Oakmont Baptist Church
Greenville, North Carolina

"*Recovering Hope for Your Church* gives congregations the needed tools to enter into a time of self-examination and discernment in order to transition from being a church going through the motions to becoming a church on the move. Hammett challenges congregations to rethink the roles of the pastor and laity, inviting us to embrace a new paradigm of leadership and shared ministry necessary for the Christian witness to be effective in today's ambiguous and 'not-religious-but-spiritual' culture. Every church can benefit from this resource!"

Ginger Howe Isom, Christ United Methodist Church
Greeneville, Tennessee

"In his new book *Recovering Hope for Your Church*, Eddie Hammett uses questions, imagery, and narrative to challenge individuals and churches 'to move the church of God forward in faith and function.' If you want to consider how to re-tool for personal and congregational transformation, check out Eddie's book today."

Ka'thy Gore Chappell, Leadership Development Coordinator
Cooperative Baptist Fellowship of North Carolina

"Eddie Hammett, consummate student of congregational life, has written an excellent and informative book for church leaders. Eddie taps into his personal medical crisis and subsequent dramatic lifestyle changes required to regain health as a metaphor for challenges congregations face today. The fact that 92-95% of churches are plateaued or declining confirms 'church infection' must be acknowledged and addressed. Most congregations have difficulty shifting their standard operating procedures. Many are content with the status quo. Hammett asserts a coach can ask good and powerful questions to awaken the consciousness of congregational leaders to the necessity of 're-formation.' Hammett's love for the church is evident on every page of his book. He is not content to simply diagnose problems facing congregations; Eddie offers practical advice, a toolbox of creative and innovative ideas, myriad lists and charts, seasoned wisdom, and stories from congregations that found spiritual vitality through engaging the coaching process. For leaders who sense their churches need spiritual infusion, *Recovering Hope for Your Church* is a must read! Be ready! You will likely find yourself in the market for a good congregational coach!"

Terry Maples, Field Coordinator
Tennessee Cooperative Baptist Fellowship

Recovering

for Your Church

Key Leadership Resources from www.TCPBooks.info

George W. Bullard Jr.
Every Congregation Needs a Little Conflict
FaithSoaring Churches
Pursuing the Full Kingdom Potential of Your Congregation

Richard L. Hamm
Recreating the Church

Edward H. Hammett
Recovering Hope for your Church:
Moving beyond Maintenance and Missional to Incarnational Engagement

Making Shifts without Making Waves:
A Coach Approach to Soulful Leadership

Reaching People under 40 while Keeping People over 60:
Being Church to All Generations

Spiritual Leadership in a Secular Age:
Building Bridges Instead of Barriers

Gregory L. Hunt
Leading Congregations through Crisis

Cynthia Woolever and Deborah Bruce
Leadership That Fits Your Church:
What Kind of Pastor for What Kind of Congregation

The Sustaining Pastoral Excellence Peer Learning Team
So Much Better:
How Thousands of Pastors Help Each Other Thrive

Larry McSwain
The Calling of Congregational Leadership:
Being, Knowing, Doing Ministry

For more leadership resources, see
www.TheColumbiaPartnership.org
www.TCPBooks.info

Recovering

for Your Church

Moving beyond Maintenance
and Missional to
Incarnational Engagement

Edward H. Hammett

Copyright ©2014 by Edward H. Hammett.

All rights reserved. For permission to reuse content, please contact Copyright Clearance Center, 222 Rosewood Drive, Danvers, MA 01923, (978) 750-8400, www.copyright.com.

Scripture quotations marked (NIV) are taken from the HOLY BIBLE, NEW INTERNATIONAL VERSION®. NIV®. Copyright © 1973, 1978, 1984 by International Bible Society. Used by permission of Zondervan Publishing House. All rights reserved.

Bible quotations marked NRSV are from the *New Revised Standard Version Bible,* copyright 1989, Division of Christian Education of the National Council of the Churches of Christ in the United States of America. Used by permission. All rights reserved.

Scripture marked NASB is taken from the *NEW AMERICAN STANDARD BIBLE®,* © Copyright The Lockman Foundation 1960, 1962, 1963, 1968, 1971, 1972, 1973, 1975, 1977, 1995. Used by permission.

Biblical quotations marked REB are from *The Revised English Bible copyright* © Oxford University Press and Cambridge University Press 1989. *The Revised English Bible with the Apocrypha* first published 1989.

Quotations marked Message are from *The Message* by Eugene H. Peterson, copyright © 1993, 1994, 1995, 1996, 2000, 2001, 2002. Used by permission of NavPress Publishing Group. All rights reserved.

Cover art: depositphotos.com
Cover design: Scribe, Inc.

Print: 978-08272-32280 EPUB: 978-08272-32297 EPDF: 978-08272-32303

Library of Congress Cataloging-in-Publication Data
Hammett, Edward H., author.
 Recovering hope for your church : from maintenance to missional and incarnational engagement / Edward H. Hammett.
 pages cm
Includes bibliographical references.
 ISBN 978-0-8272-3228-0 (pbk.)
 1. Church renewal. 2. Church. 3. Pastoral theology. 4. Hope–Religious aspects--Christianity. I. Title.

 BV600.3.H38 2014
 262.001'7–dc23

                                2014022988

www.TheColumbiaPartnership.org
www.TCPBooks.com

CONTENTS

Editor's Foreword

Inspiration and Wisdom for
21st-Century Christian Leaders

You have chosen wisely in deciding to read and learn from a book published by TCP Books from The Columbia Partnership.

We publish for

- Congregational leaders who desire to serve with greater faithfulness, effectiveness, and innovation.
- Christian ministers who seek to pursue and sustain excellence in ministry service.
- Members of congregations who desire to reach their full kingdom potential.
- Christian leaders who desire to use a coach approach in their ministry.
- Denominational and parachurch leaders who want to come alongside affiliated congregations in a servant leadership role.
- Consultants and coaches who desire to increase their learning concerning the congregations and Christian leaders they serve.

TCP Books is a sharing knowledge strategy of The Columbia Partnership, a community of Christian leaders seeking to transform the capacity of the North American Church to pursue and sustain vital Christ-centered ministry.

Primarily serving congregations, denominations, educational institutions, leadership development programs, and parachurch organizations, TCP also seeks to connect with individuals, businesses, and other organizations seeking a Christ-centered spiritual focus.

We welcome your comments on these books, and we welcome your suggestions for new subject areas and authors we ought to consider.

George Bullard, Senior Editor, TCP Books
The Columbia Partnership
332 Valley Springs Road, Columbia, SC 292236934
Voice: 803.622.0923, Website: www.TheColumbiaPartnership.org

ACKNOWLEDGMENTS

The contents of this book are a result of a lifetime of ministering on church and denominational staffs—and of consulting and coaching a host of congregations, faith communities, clergy, and lay leaders. I am deeply grateful for lessons I have been able to learn through these experiences, and the power of prayer and reflection on the experiences.

I am indebted to The Columbia Partnership and Cooperative Baptist Fellowship of North Carolina for their support, encouragement, and the opportunities for learning and fellowship I have enjoyed with each for the last five-plus years.

I too am grateful for the editing skills of Judi Hayes, who continues to contribute her wisdom, skill, and insights to make my writings clear, concise, and grammatically correct. Thanks, Judi. Your ministry is appreciated by many.

For my family, friends, and colleagues who have encouraged, challenged, and proofread, I am deeply grateful. Your support helps me continue to write and search for practical tools to move leaders and communities toward greater effectiveness.

PREFACE

The Power of Why

"EXTREME HOPES ARE BORN OF EXTREME MISERY."
—Bertrand Russell, *Unpopular Essays*

"Why?" seems to be on the lips of many church, judicatory, and denominational leaders today.

"Why has our church plateaued?"

"Why are so few young leaders going into church-based ministries?"

"Why are so few interested in church these days?"

"Why are so many churches going out of business and having to close their doors?"

"Why are the number of unchurched increasing and the number of churched decreasing?"

"Why are our churches downsizing while community spiritual needs and appetites are increasing?"

The tough economy of our day could be a gift to many churches, as it forces us to rethink, refocus, retool, and reform in order not just to survive economically but possibly to recover hope so we can thrive again in a new world. With more than four thousand churches going out of business each year in North America, and many other churches merging to prolong life, we are being forced to look at other options and retool for a new age.

Maybe the power of *why?* is found by pulling back the blanket of denial, grief, and cynicism found in many churches, judicatories, and denominations. We grieve because the good old days of the church culture are gone and cannot be recovered. We deny the reality that our declining numbers have more to do with those inside the walls of the church than those outside the walls of the church. We are cynical, if not angry, about those who are "not as committed" to the church, and those outside the walls "who do not care about God." Our fears cause us to hunker down in our safe sanctuaries and turn inward with our ministries in order to be safe and secure from the evils of the world. However, Christ calls us to be the light *in* the world, and not cover our lights under a bushel basket or hide them in the safety of sanctuaries. Our needs to be right, safe, and secure have caused many churches to become so inward focused that we are of little or no value in keeping the message of Christ alive and well in the world for which He died.

The solutions are not found so much in *why?* as in the answer to the question, *What's really going on here?* If you boiled all the realities of the church down, you would find the root of much of the stress on the church is found in the reality that some church leaders and churches are practicing more idol worship than God worship. Our idol has become "the good old days"–our "at home in Zion" feelings and experiences that we value, we treasure, we enjoy, and we are comfortable practicing. You see, it seems today's church is repeating the sin of Israel. We like who we are, and we do not plan to let anyone change us! We love our buildings, our institutions, our traditions, our style of music, our day of worship, our order of service in worship, our programs, our pews, our stained-glass windows. Yes, we love them because they mean something to *us.* In many cases our love is tied to pews, windows, buildings, organs, programs, classes, etc. These are, in turn, tied to memorials for a loved one–often complete with plaques or endowments that acknowledge the love and the gift–that prevent us from moving forward. The memories and gifts that acknowledge our earthly loves often keep us from pursuing God, who can move us into the future. God is always about creating new things, while many churches desire to hold onto the old things (2 Cor. 5:17). God keeps bringing hope for the future while we grasp tightly to experiences of the past.

Many church people are some of the church's worst enemies. These revered saints have created church in our own image, to preserve our own comfort zones. When it comes to sharing the good news of Christ with another generation, we are stuck with old plans and simplistic methods that never worked as well as we remember them working. The truth is we cannot change that which we worship, and many members worship the church more than they worship the God of the church. *We love our generation and those who have gone before so much that we may be the biggest barrier preventing*

the next generation from knowing and embracing the God of Scripture who
makes all things new (2 Cor. 5:17; Isa. 48:6).

Hope is found only when reality is embraced and the heart of
the people and the Spirit of God connect in ways that move from
struggle to hope. What will it really take to recover hope for the
church and really move the church of God forward in faith and
function?

> Moving forward calls us to be people of God, not just good
> people.
> Moving forward calls us to be people of faith, not just people
> of tradition.
> Moving forward calls us to be holy people who follow God
> rather than hollow people who are empty vessels.
> Moving forward calls us to pray without ceasing rather than
> pretending to pray so we can stay the same.
> Moving forward calls us to study Scripture to be transformed
> anew rather than symbolically studying Scripture so we can
> preserve our class fellowship and convince others we are
> spiritually mature.
> Moving forward means rediscovering and recommitting to
> why we do what we do, and for whom we do it.
> Moving forward means listening and following God rather than
> listening to sermons and being spectators in worship.

From Maintenance to
Missional to Incarnational

In the last decade we have seen many churches catch a new spirit
by moving from maintenance (inward) focus to turning outward
and becoming more missionally focused. This great effort has
helped some churches, who are now ready to face reality and move
forward, beginning a journey of renewal, refocusing, and reform.
This effort has helped shift some inward-focused values to outward-
focused experiences. Far too often, the missional effort has gotten
bogged down as folks try to discern the difference between mission
activities and missional experiences. Other churches simply treat
this as a fad, or "just changing the language," without much change
in the basic DNA of the church.

As the unchurched population increases, and the culture
continues its slide toward increasing secularization, we are being
stretched again to deepen the missional movement into an incarnational expression and commitment. We have to *earn the right*

to be heard by investing our focus, energies, and time with those who are spiritually thirsty but outside the institutional church. The church is shifting again from just the *gathered* community (*ecclesia* and *koinonia*) to the *scattered* community of salt, light, and leaven *in* the world (*diaspora*). How do the outward-focused missional experiences bear fruit that impacts and influences the growing unchurched, dechurched culture? This calls forth the incarnational elements God used when God sent His Son into the world, that the world—through Him—might be saved (Jn. 3:17). What does it mean for the scattered church to learn how to—and to become committed to—living among the poor, needy, sick, spiritually thirsty, and spiritually anemic population?

As North America becomes less churched and more spiritually thirsty, we are called to deepen our investment in people: to earn the right to be heard, to be introduced to others, and to be welcomed by the unchurched without becoming part of the unchurched. Jesus calls us to be in the world, but not of the world. Today's church faces the same challenge God faced before He sent His Son into the world. God had tried through prophets, kings, and wars to get His message across, but to no avail. Then He sent His Son, that we might know. So, how might the incarnational experience and commitment differ from missional experiences?

Incarnational experiences are captured in the INcubators of

INviting	INtroducing	INclusion
INtimacy	INvesting	INvolved

We'll look at these types of incarnational experiences throughout the book. But let's begin by comparing and contrasting the characteristics of a church with a missional focus with one that has an incarnational focus.

Henry Cloud may be onto something in his book *Necessary Endings*.[1] Cloud believes that all of us have to give up things in order to move forward: "Pruning is a process of proactive endings. It turns out that a rosebush, like many other plants, cannot reach its full potential without a very systematic process of pruning. The gardener intentionally and purposefully cuts off branches and buds that fall into any of these three categories:

1. "Healthy buds or branches that are not the best ones,
2. "Sick branches that are not going to get well, and
3. "Dead branches that are taking up space needed for the healthy ones to thrive."

MISSIONAL FOCUS	INCARNATIONAL FOCUS
Outward focused	Acceptance/Invitation focused
How do we engage people outside the walls of the church?	How do we earn acceptance and invitation into churched/unchurched relationships?
Message of influence and impact	Relational messages of reconciliation, redemption, hope, healing, and health
About being *out* among the unchurched serving humankind through relief efforts through partnerships	About being *in* with, not insulated from, persons unlike you (in but not of the world, John 17:18)
Often ask, "What can we do?"	Often ask, "Who do we need to be?"
Often ask, "How can we serve?"	Often ask, "How can we be salt, light, and leaven in this situation now?"
Committed to an assigned task of serving	Committed to walking with and living among in a way to please Christ

Cloud continues, using the pruning reality, to explore three types of necessary endings:

Necessary Ending Type 1–Pruning an overabundance of buds that the plant can not maintain effectively.

Necessary Ending Type 2–Pruning the branches that are sick or diseased and are not going to make it. At some point the observing gardener realizes that more water, more fertilizer, or more care is just not going to help. Once pruned, the plant is now fully on mission, focusing its energy every day on feeding and growing the buds that are destined to reach full bloom and maturity.

Necessary Ending Type 3–Then there are buds and branches that are dead and taking up space. The healthy branches need that room to reach their full potential.

While I realize this metaphor breaks down on several fronts when it comes to pruning of the church or churches, I do think it offers food for thought and, maybe, some next steps.

COACHING QUESTIONS

1. What needs pruning in your church? Who is responsible for recognizing the need for pruning? Who does the pruning and how?
2. What impact would pruning have in your church? your life?
3. What might the pruning look like now? in one year? in two years?
4. What are the evidences that pruning needs to happen in your church? your life?

Institutionalism and the Church

Findley B. Edge, my mentor, friend, and seminary professor, was ahead of his time when he wrote *A Quest for Vitality in Religion* and *The Greening of the Church.* Findley wrote Quest in the prosperous time of the church and declared, "Two paradoxical phenomena may be seen in the religious life of the United States today. On the one hand are numerous evidences that religion is in the midst of a period of unparalleled success. On the other, a crescendo of voices, raised both in question and warning, point up the fact that something is seriously wrong with modern Christianity."[2]

Learning from History

Findley continued to explore history and how institutionalism emerged in church life:

> A movement must be viewed not only in relation to the present but also in relation to the past... While the beginnings of three major religious movements were characterized by a vital and experiential type of religion, yet each, unaware of what was happening, went through the usual states into institutionalized forms. The first movement was Judaism from Ezra and the return of the Jews from Exile to the Pharisaism denounced during the earthly ministry of Jesus. The second movement was Christianity from the time of Jesus to the matured Roman Catholicism of the Middle Ages. The third covers the period from the Reformation under Martin Luther to the state churches in England and on the Continent.[3]

He continues to analyze each. I will not repeat it here, but rather refer you to *A Quest for Vitality in Religion.*

My sense is that the golden age of churches in the 1950s–60s and part of 1970s, while enjoyable and to some degree effective, contributed to another stage of the emerging institutionalism history has charted for us. Church buildings were built; church offices were formalized; seminaries and denominations took a strong hold on how, where, and when church was done. Then the culture began to shift, and the church focus took a backseat to a rapidly changing, unchurched culture. Church leaders, seminaries, clergy, and lay leaders lost their way amid the rapid-paced changes. Then the economy took a dive, and money slowly dried up in churches and denominations. What if these rapid-paced, deeply cutting shifts are God's way of birthing something new that works in the culture we now find ourselves in? God's mission does not change, but structures, leadership models, economic models, and ministry designs become new in order to break through institutionalism to missional and incarnational models of ministry!

The focus of *Recovering Hope for Your Church* is rooted in embracing new realities, committing to the tough road of recovery, and developing new skills, structures, and ministry designs through a process of spiritual discernment, congregational coaching of faith communities wherever they are found or emerge, and a deeper reliance on the work and ministry of the Holy Spirit. My hope is that this book will introduce a process of hope and health for churches that internal leaders or an invited congregational coach can use to discover and nurture the new life that God is birthing. I also pray that the tools and framework presented will encourage, guide, and inspire pastors, leaders, churches, denominations, and judicatories to believe that recovery of hope is possible. If readers need additional help or coaching in this process, we at Transforming Solutions have coaches ready to awaken the hope in you or your congregation. The road of recovery is a personal and spiritual journey for me, and this is likely to be true for you and your church. Let's journey together and see what new discoveries God has for us now. You can also find ongoing updates, coaching tools, and powerful stories of insights from the journey of others on my personal website www.TransformingSolutions.org.

PART I

Finding Hope for Your Church

explores...

- When Infection/Lies Enter the Body
- Lies Many Churches Believe
- Uncovering Blind Spots and Lies Leaders Perpetuate
- Scope of Transitions Facing Churches

Different Members in One Body

"NOW FAITH IS CONFIDENCE IN WHAT WE HOPE FOR AND
ASSURANCE ABOUT WHAT WE DO NOT SEE.
THIS IS WHAT THE ANCIENTS WERE COMMENDED FOR."
—Hebrews 11:1–2, NIV

Christ is like a single body with its many limbs and organs, which, many as they are, together make up one body; for in the one Spirit we were all brought into one body by baptism, whether Jews or Greeks, slaves or free; we were all given that one Spirit to drink.

A body is not a single organ, but many. Suppose the foot were to say, "Because I am not a hand, I do not belong to the body," it belongs to the body none the less. Suppose the ear were to say, "Because I am not an eye, I do not belong to the body," it still belongs to the body. If the body were all eye, how could it hear? If the body were all ear, how could it smell? But, in fact, God appointed each limb and organ to its own place in the body as he chose. If the whole were a single organ, there would not be a body at all; in fact, however, there are many different organs, but one body. The eye cannot say to the hand, "I do not need you," or the head to the feet, "I do not need you." Quite the contrary: those parts of the body which seem to be more frail than others are indispensable, and those parts of the body which we regard as less honourable are treated with special honour. The parts we are modest about are treated with special respect, whereas our respectable parts have no such need. But God has combined the various parts of the body, giving special honour to the humbler parts, so that there might be no division in the body, but that all its parts might feel the same concern for one another. If one part suffers, all suffer together; if one flourishes, all rejoice together.

Now you are Christ's body, and each of you a limb or organ of it. Within our community God has appointed in the first place apostles, in the second place prophets, thirdly teachers; then miracle-workers, then those who have gifts of healing, or ability to help others or power to guide them, or the gift of tongues of various kinds. Are all apostles? All prophets? All teachers? Do all work miracles? Do all have gifts of healing? Do all speak in tongues of ecstasy? Can all interpret them? The higher gifts are those you should prize.

But I can show you an even better way.

—1 Corinthians 12:12–31, REB

1

When Infection/Lies Enter the Body

THE IMPACT OF LIES ON THE CHURCH

"HOPE IS THE THING WITH FEATHERS,
THAT PERCHES IN THE SOUL,
AND SINGS THE TUNE WITHOUT THE WORDS,
AND NEVER STOPS AT ALL..."
—Emily Dickinson, "Hope Is the Thing with Feathers"

No doubt the essence of hope is found in God. The roots of hope for the church are found in God. The challenge for many churches today is acknowledging and following God rather than traditions or personal preferences. An authentic church of God will always have hope. Is your church God's church or is it structured and functioning around your desires and preferences rather than God's? That is a key question this book will help you explore and resolve.

Hope is often found when reality is embraced. What happens when an infection enters and drains the energy from your local church, the body of Christ? How does such an infection impact the church? How can a church recover once the infection of untruths, limiting beliefs, and lies have entered the life and ministries of a church? God has used a personal health struggle to teach me about infection and how elements contrary to a healthy body rob the body of energy, influence, life, and health. God continues to teach me, and this book is an attempt to share some of my learnings with churches that find themselves losing life, influence, and health.

3

So many churches are at best limping these days; weakness and dis-ease of members brings many churches to self-service, inward focus, weakness of influence, and being permeated by signs of fleeting life—decline in membership, finances, rundown buildings in need of repair, multiple programs void of member participation.

These questions have a personal meaning for me for various reasons. In January 2007, I had open-heart surgery to replace my heart valve that had been eaten and destroyed by a staph infection that, unbeknown to me, had entered my blood stream. I had been warned, ever since discovering I was born with a bad valve, that one day this valve would likely need to be replaced or repaired. Delaying such an invasive surgery seemed wise, since the valve was giving me little difficulty when it was discovered. Delaying such a life-threatening operation sounded good to me, but, even better, technology was advancing significantly, and the longer I waited the more likely I could benefit from cutting-edge discoveries and surgical procedures. However, I was warned that I should be careful even during dental procedures and other surgical-type procedures. Taking antibiotics before the procedures would greatly reduce the possibility of bacteria getting into that valve and creating trouble.

I lived for almost thirty years after diagnosis without any major challenges. Then, somewhere in my travels I encountered a staph infection, and it slowly but surely destroyed my heart valve to the point it could not be repaired and had to be replaced.

The valve had been destroyed by an infection that secretly entered my body and gradually weakened the heart muscle that brought me life, breath, and energy every minute of every day. As the heart valve decayed, I lost energy, became lightheaded, had a high fever and intense and consistent chills, lost appetite, and was so weak that a shower wiped me out for the day! My doctor treated me for flu-like symptoms to begin with, but we discovered after two rounds of antibiotics something else was going on. A battery of tests revealed I had a serious staph infection. The heart surgeon would not even talk with me until the infection had been destroyed. Surgery would have been high risk otherwise. So for six weeks I received two intravenous treatments of high-powered antibiotics per day. Wow, talk about pummeling a body! The antibiotics zapped me. What little energy I had, the meds took it! I was so weakened that I was in solitude, except for medical care, for about eight weeks. The solitude of that time became a real source of inner transformation. Life took on a very different perspective; mine was slipping away, and I knew it.

Permit me to highlight in an abbreviated way some issues I have lived through that I believe have something to say to the body of Christ infected by lies.

SIGNS OF POSSIBLE INFECTION IN THE BODY

1. Growing fatigue
2. Inability to focus
3. Feverish
4. Withdrawn
5. Resistant and unresponsive to standard treatments
6. Fluctuating vital signs
7. Lack of appetite
8. Inactivity
9. Inability to rest well

TYPICAL TREATMENT FOR ENHANCED INFECTIONS

1. Rest, rest, and more rest
2. Intravenous fluids and high-priced, powerful prescription cocktail of antibiotics
3. Skilled, consistent supervisory medical care and help with daily routine
4. Reflection and solitude
5. Maximized energy for must-do daily essential activities–basics
6. Monitoring vital signs daily
7. Periodic evaluation–blood work

I could write a book about each of these physical, emotional, spiritual, and mental challenges; but, suffice it to say, the body goes through a slow period of deterioration once infection enters–so slow that, sometimes, you barely notice it. Then one day the bottom falls out, and reality hits! Treatment releases the physical body, mind, and spirit to go through a methodical, slow, often anguishing time of recovery as direction, stamina, and focus are gradually restored. Such a journey cannot be done alone. It demands facing realities, practicing intentionality, focus, prayer, reflection, and seeking knowledgeable guidance.

I know a church, in fact, several churches, that have faced similar challenges. One UMC church struggled amidst a changing neighborhood and an aging membership, with no children and leaders with little resources to keep the church going. The pastor was serving three congregations, and she was so stressed with all the pastoral care needs that she had very little time or energy to lead the church forward. The apathy and deterioration of leadership and resources were certainly taking their toll. The pastor and two key leaders then caught a fresh vision of how their small struggling church could partner with area churches and agencies to more effectively serve their congregation *and* their community. Now, that once-dying church is thriving because a few caught a new vision and were willing to make some shifts in behavior, and focus. Recovering hope is possible but it takes some shifts and determination.

I believe the lists in the next chapter accurately depict the lies/infections that have invaded many churches today. Such lies/infections are draining the life from our clergy and lay leaders. Such infections are distracting churches from God's mission and causing many to turn inward in an attempt to sustain the churches themselves. These infectious lies have robbed many contemporary religious groups of all hope for the future. They stand paralyzed by the present. What do you think?

2

Lies Many Churches Believe

FOUR CATEGORIES THAT CAN KILL CHURCHES

"HOPE IS WHAT KEEPS YOU GOING,
BUT HOPE KEEPS YOU FOCUSED ON THE FUTURE,
AND THIS CONTINUED FOCUS PERPETUATES YOUR DENIAL
OF THE NOW AND THEREFORE YOUR UNHAPPINESS."
—Eckhard Tolle, *The Power of Now*

A variety of recent books address lies in the church. These represent a shift in church leadership literature in the last five years. My review of these books brought me some affirmation that other church leaders are seeing the same trends. On the other hand, my review also brings to my heart a deep ache for those leaders working in this overwhelming environment. I also found little agreement on solutions to the lies at work in our leaders and churches. My attempt is to provide a coach approach to allow leaders and congregations to explore, discern, and discover collaboratively those issues that inhibit God's mission from being manifest in their churches.

As you review my categories and listing of lies, begin your self-assessment. Read it as a leader, then read it considering your church. Mark all that apply. We will work with these later in the book. What is the reality God is presenting to you now? What might the journey of recovering hope look like? Consider:

BELIEFS

CATEGORY 1. LIES THAT DISTRACT

Returning to the good old days is the way forward for our church.

Ministry is for the church members to support and pray for, but not something they are to do.

Being good people is as vital as being God's people.

If we build a family life center with a gym, young families with children will flock to our church.

A good pastor will visit all the homebound households once per month.

If we start a second worship service, we will split the church.

There are plenty of our kind of people in this community for us to have a really good church.

CATEGORY 2. LIES THAT DISCOURAGE

The newsletter and annual report describe who we are.

Those who are not like us should not be invited or encouraged be among us or part of us.

Judging others is essential if the church is to stay pure and faithful.

Using most of our resources to maintain classes, buildings, committees, ministries, and programs is a way of honoring our pastor and preserving our future.

Adults do not want to serve.

Volunteers do not want to be trained!

God only calls men into leadership and ministry.

If we get rid of our current pastor, we will like the next one better.

BEHAVIORS

CATEGORY 3. LIES THAT DESTROY

Church meetings, ministries, and programs are primarily to accommodate the needs and preferences of church members rather than those inactive or beyond the membership.

Caregiving for members is the primary mission of the church.

The budget of the church is for those who give, not for those who do not give or come to church.

New members must attend here for at least two years before we can let them lead something, five to ten years before they can have any key roles in the church.

We do not need to do background checks on anyone; we know
   everybody here.

Funding for ministry for our church comes only from the tithes
   and offerings of members and guests.

As a church we are more faithful if we preserve the past than if
   we create the future.

We do not need a stewardship emphasis because everyone is
   already giving all they can.

Endowments secure the future of our church

CATEGORY 4. LIES THAT DIMINISH IMPACT/INFLUENCE

Ministry is the primary responsibility of the pastor and staff.

To be a faithful church we must be found doing the same thing,
   at the same time, and in the same place.

Measuring attendance is the primary indicator of the effectiveness of our church.

Preserving doctrinal purity and denominational alignment
   is essential if the church is to move forward in faith and
   function.

Doctrine is more important than leadership and vision drivers
   in designing an effective church.

Adding a youth or children's minister to the staff will grow the
   church and ensure its future.

The challenge of churches and leaders is how to correct the
lies or move on from them to be more effective in God's mission through our churches and personal ministry. I worked with
a congregation bound by their lies and experienced an unfolding
of new energy, vision, and truth as they walked into their lies:
Lies that they were too small, too white, too affluent to reach their
transitioning neighborhood. After much soul searching, dialogue,
prayer, and work, they planted a community garden as an en-
trée to their hungry community. The relationships that emerged
through this one act made new relationships, new visions, and
renewed motivation.

   I use the following exercise as a way of beginning to move from
the lies that bind to corrected lies that launch into more effective
ministry. Use the worksheet below to continue listing and processing
what needs to happen to you and the church now to move forward.

From Lies to Launching More Effective Ministry

Use the chart below to record your responses to the following
questions:

1. What distorted truths or limiting beliefs prevent your church from moving forward?
2. How can this be corrected? Who in the church is in position to show these lies to the congregation?
3. Which three lies corrected can be converted to launch pads to ensure more effective ministry now?

IDENTIFIED LIES/ LIMITING BELIEFS	WHAT WILL IT TAKE TO CORRECT OUR LIES?	WHAT DOES THE LAUNCH LOOK LIKE?

COACHING QUESTIONS
1. What did this exercise say to you?
2. What are the next steps you need to take? Who will lead in this first step?
3. How many others in your church need to work on this exercise?
4. How can you share this information with them?

3

Uncovering
Blind Spots and
Lies Leaders
Perpetuate

"A MAN BEGINS TO DIE WHEN HE CEASES TO
EXPECT ANYTHING FROM TOMORROW."
—Abraham Miller, *Unmoral Maxims*

Facing harsh realities is often the first step to treatment and then recovery. Many churches are crying for leadership in a day of fast-paced change, seismic cultural shifts, increasing demographic changes, and pluralism that often fuels their downward spin of effectiveness and participation. Though some churches (and denominations) are aware of these realities, they are often not willing to pay the high price of change—often because they acquaint change with unfaithfulness to God. Anchored in the concrete of tradition, ritual, and comfort zones, congregations—and too often leaders of congregations (both clergy and laity)—have blind spots and intentionally or unintentionally perpetuate lies that contribute to the church's ineffectiveness and plateaued state rather than leading them forward. But honesty fuels hope.

In my own health challenges, I was blind and in denial of the truth that my decreasing energy and increasing fatigue were symptoms of something worse than a busy schedule or a flu bug. I finally went to the doctor with a high temperature that I couldn't ignore, and his treatments began. But, at first his practice of medicine brought only temporary relief to a much deeper issue.

Discovering blind spots of leaders and congregations is tough and typically demands an outsider as well. Outsiders, with no agenda and no familiarity with the church culture or leaders' style, can fairly quickly discover blind spots and weaknesses in leadership style. After a couple of hours of focused conversations with key leaders and a walk through facilities, a good congregational coach or consultant can begin to see and/or experience blind spots. Some possible discovery questions might include:

1. What are you celebrating as a result of the last year of ministry in this setting?
2. What three challenges do you face consistently?
3. How do you typically deal with the challenges?
4. What is the typical result of your response to these consistent challenges?
5. What are your goals for the future? As pastor and church?

Such a conversation typically reveals leadership patterns and at least points toward some possible blind spots or leadership deficits or strengths.

Why would a leader or church do this? Most congregations do not want to change. Mike Regele's book, *Death of the Church*, can be summarized in one sentence: Most churches would rather die than change.[1] Many leaders choose to perpetuate a congregation or denomination's lies to preserve the leaders' sanity and minimize resistance of their members who provide the source of funds that fuels the institution and pays their salaries.

Findley Edge wrote of this problem of institutionalism in his pioneering book, *A Quest for Vitality in Religion*, published in 1963.[2] Pioneer writers have explored this very issue for decades, and yet churches and denominations refuse to change—not to change simply to change, but to change so that the new culture we find ourselves in might be able to hear, receive, and respond to the good news of the gospel and discover anew God's work in this world.

A county seat town congregation faced their lies and discovered their ministry. Though the challenge was not easy, it was possible. Most of their church business sessions had been dominated by budgets, buildings, and reports on the pastor. A fresh vision and some key leaders willing to step into the new vision created a shift in the business meetings. They reported on what God was doing in their community through the ministries of feeding the hungry, clothing the needy, and tutoring children in the local school. The change in reporting shifted the inward focused agenda to an outward focused missional agenda. They will likely never be that inward focused congregation again!

What are some of the lies leaders perpetuate, more through behaviors than cognitive beliefs? Why do they maintain these lies? Is it in order to preserve their sanity while serving congregations that do not embrace the need or the challenge to change? Many leaders know better when it comes to these untruths, but because many churches (and denominations) are so entrenched and cherish their longstanding practices, pastors and key lay leaders choose not to fight the battle or rock the boat. Trying to correct false beliefs almost certainly creates opposition, stress, and hostility, if not open conflict, in a church/denomination. The pastor and others say, "It is just not worth the risk and chaos." This attitude and fear of conflict perpetuate the cycle of dysfunction, ineffectiveness, and immobilizing beliefs and behaviors that are leading our churches into a state of despair, decline, and ultimately demise of impact in our culture.

While it seems I am blaming leaders, I certainly understand their fears and concerns. Even as I type these words, I wonder what conflict–pushback–my statements might create once read by those most in need of help in their churches. But for the sake of security and peace, leaders are guilty of perpetuating the lies listed in chapter 2.

Much of the way leaders perpetuate these lies in the fabric of congregational life is by leaning more toward a pastoral care model than a pastoral leadership model within the culture of the congregation/denomination. Most congregations and denominations gravitate to pastoral care (caring for the saints through spiritual formation for their nurture and being attentive when they are wounded, sick, bereaved, or in crisis). While this breeds trust and relationships, too much of this model often turns congregations into vehicles of maintenance rather than vehicles of mission. The church has become so inward focused that it has lost its impact, respect, and influence in the broken world for which the church was created in the first place. We must remind ourselves, "God so loved the *world*, that He gave..." (Jn. 3:16, NASB, emphasis added). The world, not necessarily the church, was God's focus.

4

Scope of Transitions Facing Churches

TYING HISTORY TO HOPE
(WHERE IN THE WORLD IS YOUR CHURCH?)

"HOPE IS LIKE THE SUN, WHICH, AS WE JOURNEY TOWARDS IT,
CASTS THE SHADOW OF OUR BURDEN BEHIND US...
IT LENDS PROMISE TO THE FUTURE AND PURPOSE TO THE PAST.
IT TURNS DISCOURAGEMENT TO DETERMINATION."
—Samuel Smiles, *Self-Help*

Diagnosis often begins with a series of questions to explore symptoms—whether in the physical body or the church body. What do you think when asked, "Where in the world is your church?"? Do you respond with a street address of your church facilities? Do you think of all the places your church sponsors missionaries as an extension of your ministry? Or do you think of all the places your members work, attend school, play on sports teams, or participate in community leadership or community-wide events?

Your response to the question tells a lot about how you and your congregation define *church*. Do you see church as a place you *go* for worship and equipping, or do you see church as the body dispersed throughout the city as representatives of Christ seeking to be salt, light, and leaven in the world? During a church culture era (prior to 1960), many saw church as "gathered," a place to assemble. Today, in a post-Christendom culture, we are learning to be both—the gathered and the scattered church. The scattered church comes from Acts 2, when the apostles scattered (were dispersed) throughout the city.

The twenty-first–century church that desires to impact and influence the world for Christ is moving beyond the missional movement to an incarnational movement. The incarnational church sees its members focused on *being church* rather than just *going to church*. For most members today, church life typically happens within the church walls, programs, and membership. The life of the incarnational church happens as the presence, grace, and mercy of Christ are experienced in the world as light encounters darkness, hope encounters pain, and encouragement pushes back despair. We are being called out to learn to be salt, light, and leaven in ways that influence and impact the culture of unchurched persons we work with each day.

What is needed for this type of church to be effective in witness, impact, and influence? What type of leadership styles are needed to mobilize the saints in the pews into the streets of the city? What type of structures, curricula, rituals, and traditions are needed to focus on being the presence of Christ in the increasingly secular world? These are challenging and significant questions today's church leaders and congregations must not ignore.

One church I have worked with identifies itself in their monthly newsletter as "serving as priests in the world." They celebrate "one lady who works in Randolph Courthouse who is assembling a small group of interested people at 7:30 a.m. on Thursdays to pray for the people who work and enter the courthouse." Additionally, the pastor celebrates two teachers who "last year...met together every Monday morning at the school where they teach to pray for the school, students and faculty." Another office manager incorporates a devotion into her monthly staff meetings. These are simple but powerful examples of incarnational ministry in the world as the church.

G. Jeffrey MacDonald, in his article "Who's in the Pews?" reviews the seismic shifts happening in church life in New England. He explains: "The Ark (a new faith community in New England) is symbolic of a transforming religious landscape in New England and may be an indicator of the future of American religion. Long defined by dominate Roman Catholic and mainline Protestant institutions, the terrain is undergoing a fundamental shift as traditional denominations cope with steep declines in membership and shutter churches and seminaries." He continues by declaring: "The old establishment is crumbling in the sense that fewer people are going to church and buildings are being sold off... The old expectations are not there anymore and that creates an openness to new brands." He summarizes these shifts by explaining:

> What's emerging, it seems, is a religious shift whose wider meaning is best measured not so much in terms of political or cultural transformation, but in how faith is practiced. Adherents are flocking to churches where the difference faith makes is concrete and visible. Connections focused in faith communities are enabling them to live in keeping with their aspirations and nurture freedoms they've come to discover... Hope for the church is not found in programs, pastors, or preserving the past. Hope for the church demands discovering and embracing practical ways of fueling faith and sustaining spiritual formation. Such hope remains rooted in New Testament truth that transforms the lay and clergy leaders while forging evolving structures to serve, redeem, and reconcile others.[1]

A congregational coach can help congregations do a self-assessment of all the changes swirling around them personally, their families, their communities, and their culture. The list that follows provides a synopsis of some of the most prevalent transitions many churches are facing now and will face in the coming years. The coach can distribute the list early in the coaching experience and ask each person to put checkmarks beside all the issues that resonate personally with them, then ask them to circle the issues touching the congregation now, and finally ask them to put stars beside all they sense will impact their church/community in the next three to five years. Following this exercise, the coach can encourage them to share responses in small groups and prepare to bring the top five issues to the large-group conversation. The coach then leads the group to prioritize these transitional issues as to which are most important for the church to pay attention to now so as to move the congregation forward and prepare for the future. Listing these conclusions provides a great backdrop for further conversations.

SCOPE OF TRANSITIONS FACING CHURCHES IN 2014–2020

ECONOMIC ISSUES
National economic problems
Local economic changes
Church funding sources/changes

LOCAL TOWN ISSUES
Demographics (population characteristics)
Growing unchurched population

TECHNOLOGICAL ISSUES
Purchasing plans
Access issues
Training programs
Areas and times of usage

CHURCH PROGRAM ISSUES
Time available to disciple adults
Meeting relationship and cultural differences
Time and training needs of differing generations
New definitions of family and personal relationships
Programming worship to meet differing tastes
Diversity in curriculum needs for Bible study and discipling
Ministering to people with differing learning styles
Use of locally produced programs and emphases, independent
    publishers' materials, or denominational materials
Scheduling in light of secularizing of Sabbath and work schedules
Formation and function of short-term leadership teams
Downsizing/streamlining programming
Creating and functioning in collaborative partnerships

CHURCH ORGANIZATIONAL ISSUES
Demographics (diversity of membership)
Staffing changes
Creating sacred space and time
Choice and training of organizational leaders
Selection, training, roles, and responsibility of deacons/elders/
    etc.
Creating dreams for the future and selling the dreams
Maintaining the present while dreaming and implementing
    dreams of future

CHURCH MISSION ISSUES
Mission trip planning and funding
Local mission projects
Parachurch project support and participation
Denominational mission programs
Communicating the gospel by changing church in the changing
    culture
Making visits or connecting locally

NATIONAL ISSUES
   Secularism
   Skepticism

WHAT ELSE?

COACHING QUESTIONS
   1. What does this exercise say to you?
   2. What is missing from this list?
   3. What other leaders or members need to complete the exercise?
   4. When and how should you share your results with others?

Exploring shifts that are happening in our culture and how they are impacting the way we do church is a way of self-assessment, clarifying our man-made methods without compromising our God-given message and mandate. Consider the "Shifts Happening That Impact Church" chart that follows.

DIRECTIONS
   1. Circle all, in any column, that resonate with you personally.
   2. Place checkmarks beside all items in any column that your church is acknowledging and acting on.
   3. Put an asterisk (*) beside any item you feel would be a viable next step for your congregation to help move you forward in effectiveness. Share your results with key leaders and ask, "How can we take a next step on a few of these issues in the next six months?"

Shifts Happening That Impact Church

EVAPORATING	EMERGING	POSSIBLE IMPACT
Landline phones	Increase of mobile phones	Mobility/connection/ delivery system option for Christian education
Denominational alignment	Multiple alignments	Partnership building surpasses denominational building
Maintenance-minded churches	Missional-focused churches	Church presence more valued than church attendance
Inward-focused evaluation metrics	Missional/outward-focused evaluation metrics	Measuring church by impact and influence, not just attendance

Clergy-driven church	Lay-driven ministries	Celebrating all the people of God and church in the world
Eight-hour workday/five days a week	24–7 work week	Multiple programming at times and places most accessible and convenient
Economic base stressed due to aging congregation	Diversified financial base	Using creative funding sources, technological venues for giving/supporting
Leadership base for ongoing programming	Short-term teams for short-term programs	Missional-focused experiences led by missional teams
Print media	Digital and multiple delivery systems for multiple cultures and languages	Multiple delivery systems designed to communicate for understanding, engagement, and interaction
Church facility base that defines church	Church mission focus that defines church	Decentralized campuses with less focus on facility and more focus on impact
Staff-/choir-led worship	Lay-led, rotating leadership teams for worship	Collaborative worship planning and leadership models emerge
Single baptismal practices dictated by polity	Open baptism practices based on calling, commissioning	Baptism becomes celebration and commissioning for the incarnational presence of the church in the world
Teacher-led, time-bound Bible study groups	Leader team-led, dispersed small groups	Coach approach to adult Bible study in communities, workplaces, and church gatherings
Denominationally focused and distributed curricula	Curricula design and selection from various sources in keeping with church mission	Curricula designed, written, and delivered by regional teams, digital delivery only
Congregational-based church	Missional-based church	Multiple forms (including Internet delivery) of church gatherings and impact
Televisions are disappearing in many homes	On-demand mobile television programming and movies	Entertainment, education, leisure becoming on demand and mobile

PART II

Activating Hope in Your Church

explores...

- From Lies to Launching More Effective Ministry
- When Spiritual Formation Is Not Enough
- What Is Distinctive about Missional Leadership?
- Moving from Maintenance to Missional to Incarnational Engagement
- Bullying in the Church and What to Do about It

To Be Mature

In light of all this, here's what I want you to do. While I'm locked up here, a prisoner for the Master, I want you to get out there and walk—better yet, run!—on the road God called you to travel. I don't want any of you sitting around on your hands. I don't want anyone strolling off, down some path that goes nowhere. And mark that you do this with humility and discipline—not in fits and starts, but steadily, pouring yourselves out for each other in acts of love, alert at noticing differences and quick at mending fences.

You were all called to travel on the same road and in the same direction, so stay together, both outwardly and inwardly. You have one Master, one faith, one baptism, one God and Father of all, who rules over all, works through all, and is present in all. Everything you are and think and do is permeated with Oneness.

But that doesn't mean you should all look and speak and act the same. Out of the generosity of Christ, each of us is given his own gift. The text for this is,

> He climbed the high mountain,
> He captured the enemy and seized the booty,
> He handed it all out in gifts to the people.

Is it not true that the One who climbed up also climbed down, down to the valley of earth? And the One who climbed down is the One who climbed back up, up to highest heaven. He handed out gifts above and below, filled heaven with his gifts, filled earth with his gifts. He handed out gifts of apostle, prophet, evangelist, and pastor-teacher to train Christ's followers in skilled servant work, working within Christ's body, the church, until we're all moving rhythmically and easily with each other, efficient and graceful in response to God's Son, fully mature adults, fully developed within and without, fully alive like Christ.

No prolonged infancies among us, please. We'll not tolerate babes in the woods, small children who are an easy mark for impostors. God wants us to grow up, to know the whole truth and tell it in love—like Christ in everything. We take our lead from Christ, who is the source of everything we do. He keeps us in step with each other. His very breath and blood flow through us, nourishing us so that we will grow up healthy in God, robust in love. (Ephesians 4:1–16, *The Message*)

5

From Lies to Launching a More Effective Ministry

SELF-ASSESSMENT FOR PLATEAUED CHURCHES

"THERE IS NO MEDICINE LIKE HOPE, NO INCENTIVE SO GREAT
AND NO TONIC SO POWERFUL AS EXPECTATION OF
SOMETHING BETTER TOMORROW."
—Orison Sweet Marden, *He Can Who Thinks He Can*

Sometimes self-assessment and self-treatment are not enough to eliminate the infectious disease in the body. My personal journey took me to a number of specialists who put me through a battery of tests to diagnose my ailment. I did not enjoy the tests but was really too weak to fight them. I was just grateful for some help. When the diagnosis and prognosis were finally given, I was stunned; but the serious and life-challenging/threatening treatment was the only option I had because my life was slipping away rapidly. The doctors gathered and conferred and declared I had a chance, but I faced serious treatments, heart surgery, and a tough recovery.

Facing reality—by leaders, churches, and/or denominations—is a first step of correcting the lies, embracing truth, and launching into more effective ministry in our increasingly secular and broken world. About 92–95 percent of the churches in North America are plateaued or declining in attendance. My observation, as a local church staff member, denominational employee, and church and clergy coach for the past thirty years is that most of these churches are plateaued and stuck because the expectation and focus are primarily on caregiving for the members rather than leading the church to move forward in a more effective ministry. Many pastors want to vision and lead the church forward, but the expectation of the members is that they care more than they lead.

In fact, many in the congregation do not want the pastor to vision or lead because those in the pew might have to change, and they do not want that! So pastors and other leaders find themselves in a real pinch, and in a no-win scenario. (I discuss this challenge at length in *Reaching People Under 40 While Keeping People Over 60.*) In churches with an average attendance of more than one hundred, pastors realize that if they do not care (visit hospitals, nursing homes, home visits, funeral homes, etc.), they are criticized. If they do all that is expected in caring, they have little or no time or energy left to vision, pray, preach well, or take care of themselves and their families, much less lead the church to penetrate the community with the gospel of Christ. The truth is that many churches with average attendance of one hundred or less are small because they do not make needed shifts in expectations or skills of their pastor and leaders. They stay small because they design it that way, intentionally or unintentionally. What can a pastor and church do?

Facing Reality and Launching a New Direction

A church that has plateaued numerically, is stuck spiritually, or finds itself irrelevant to many people needs to ask:

- Are we expecting our pastor/staff (and lay leaders) to care to such a degree that we limit time and energy the pastor/staff and leaders have to vision, lead, and move us forward?
- What would happen if we freed our pastor/staff up from so much caregiving and blessed them to vision, lead, and move us forward?
- How can we realign our expectations for caregiving to free up our leaders?
- What's the possibility of shifting some of the time pastors/staff spend on caregiving to leading (eg., shifting from visitation three or four times a week to once a week, with other visits made by members of the church on behalf of the pastor/staff, so more time is freed up for leaders to vision, etc.)?
- What will happen to our church when members assume more of the caregiving and pastor/staff are freed to vision, pray, innovate, and lead?

- What will members and pastor/staff need to do to move our church to the next level of faith and effectiveness?
- Are we willing to pay this price and make these shifts?
- What are the consequences if we do not make these shifts?

Calling Forth Missional Leaders—Moving from Maintenance to Missional Leadership

My hope is that this chapter might stimulate some thinking and dialogue around the issues listed above so that you will discover ways of leading your church off the plateau and on to the mountain top. A church where I recently spoke did not like my message related to this theme, but they started talking about these critical issues for the first time in decades. One of the members later called me and said, "We really did not like what you said, but it helped us move from denial and begin to struggle with tough issues we know we must address if our church is to have a vital future."

Providing tools for leaders, churches, and denominations is a first step to God's plan and desire for the church and the world. *Moving from denial through fears to face truths, not perceptions and traditions, is a way forward.* Explore these distinctives of missional leadership as compared to traditional leadership. Where are you? What shifts might God be calling you/your church to make now? Cooperative Baptist Fellowship's Dawnings: Welcoming a New Day in Your Church's Missional Journey (www.cbfdawnings.org) provides a great leadership retreat framework to deepen a church's spiritual formation and sensitivity to the Spirit's leading.

Missional leadership has some major differences from a traditional leadership model. The chart below gives a glimpse of my learnings about missional leadership distinctives. A church's leaders model behaviors that guide (formally or informally) a church's direction. Incarnational leadership goes to a deeper level that I will address later in the book.

DIRECTIONS

1. Circle all that speak to you of your personal leadership model/behaviors.
2. Put asterisks (*) beside items that illustrate your general church behaviors.
3. What does this say to you?

What Is Distinctive about Missional Leadership?

LEADERSHIP BEHAVIORS	TRADITIONAL LEADERS	MISSIONAL LEADERS
Visioning	Keeping members/ maintaining tradition/ rituals	Mobilizing members to engage community as believers
Planning	Designing programming/ ministry for members	Creating partnerships and channels for engaging the unchurched
Modeling/Mentoring	Creating church leaders that value traditional means/methods	Mobilizing leaders to penetrate the community as the incarnational presence of Christ
Caregiving	Nurturing, caring for needs of members	Equipping members to care for one another and those in their sphere of influence in the world
Preaching/teaching	To instruct in the faith, to attend worship and church programs, to be "good people"	To equip, inspire, and celebrate the ministry of the church in the world
Evaluation markers	How many are faithful to church attendance via "come structures" (events at the church facilities)	The impact and influence of the members in their families, workplaces, and community thru "go structures" (experiences beyond the church facilities)
Use of time	Focused on members	Focused on members and community in keeping with demographics
Community involvement	Church family	Beyond church members/attendees
Partnering for ministry	With other churches and church leaders to engage members in church life	With other churches and community groups to engage members in church life and community life
Giving/stewardship	Raising funds to support staffing, facilities, and programs for church family	Providing variety of avenues of giving of gifts, talents, and finances to improve the presence and impact of the church in the world

COACHING QUESTIONS

1. What shifts are being called for to improve your missional impact?
2. What will help this happen?
3. Who needs to be involved?
4. How can we make this happen?

Every leader and every church have preferred leadership styles. The prevalent style is usually the one you most observe or the extreme opposite rather than the leadership style that is unique to you, based on gifts, callings, and context for ministry. Over the years I have watched my leadership style shift depending on the context and demands of the ministry in which I was engaged. I have also observed, in myself and through my coaching, that vision comes from and goes to a variety of places based on which leadership style is operative. Consider the chart:

1. What resonates with you?
2. What represents your comfort zone?
3. What might be the benefit or consequence of shifting?

Where Does Your Vision Come from and Where Is It Going?

BENEFITS OF LEADERSHIP THAT...

Casts Vision	Calls Forth Vision
Clear and direct	Fuzzy, indirect
Offer challenge	Offer/invite ownership
Command respect and accountability	Earn respect and invite accountability
Push to desired outcomes	Create pull to owned outcomes
Appoint leaders	Generate leadership for vision

CHALLENGES OF LEADERSHIP THAT...

Casts Vision	Calls Forth Vision
Builds unity of focus/action	Requires time, patience, discernment, and perseverance
Communicates and builds ownership among majority	Communicates, creating trust among majority
Creates atmosphere for adoption and supportive vote	Creates collaborative atmosphere
Tells leaders what will happen and what to expect	Invites leaders to explore and determine what the future holds and what is needed to make it happen
Keeps the pressure on to ensure alignment to adopted vision	Continually invites openness to voices of members and the Spirit

COACHING QUESTIONS

1. Which category chart speaks to you? to your church? Circle it.
2. What does this say about you? about your church?
3. What are the implications?
4. What is the Spirit saying?

The type of leader you are or that a church embraces often determines the level of conflict that emerges, the level of ownership of dreams that occurs, and the level of involvement of members. The more leaders function as missional leaders, rather than traditional leaders, the greater the chances of a church moving into a missional zone. Living in a missional zone includes the following characteristics. Evaluate how you and your church align with these characteristics. What is needed to improve your missional ministry? What is needed to take you to the next level of being an incarnational leader and church? Self-evaluation and self-honesty are key ingredients for anybody facing diagnosis, treatment, and recovery.

Being in the Missional Zone

ACTS 2:42–45

When a church is in the missional zone, what is it doing?

- It intentionally manifests fruit and gifts of the Spirit wherever believers are present.
- Believers show up as an intentional, incarnational presence of Christ.
- The church functions not just as a location of worshipers but also as a people of impact and influence in the community at large.
- Ministry is done by and expected from all of the members and not just from the paid clergy.
- Programs and ministries are planned and conducted primarily as vehicles of ministry to those yet unreached by the church, and as vehicles for believers to serve.
- The scattered church is at least of equal value to the expression of church and faithfulness as is the gathered church.
- Church effectiveness and success are determined by the impact and influence of the church on the community and culture in which it shows up and not just by those who attend activities or worship.

- Stewardship is more about generous and cheerful giving to others than maintaining facilities or programs just for believers/members.
- Leadership is equally seen and accountable for being *in* the church, serving *through* the church, and *representing* Christ and the church in the world.
- Functions and forms of church are at least equally focused on *outward* as *inward* expressions of ministry

COACHING QUESTIONS TO EXPLORE

1. Which statements best describe your church's belief system and practice?
2. What does this say about who you are as church?
3. How do people outside the fellowship see your church?

Leadership style emerges from spiritual formation framework and one's value system as well as skill set. Recovering health and hope depends on diagnosis and treatment from a physical but also from a spiritual perspective. Let's explore how a church's view of spiritual formation and pastoral care impacts their ability to be a missional and incarnational faith community.

6

When Spiritual Formation Is Not Enough

GIVING HOPE A FRAMEWORK

"THE SEASON OF BEREAVEMENT
BECOMES THE SEED-TIME OF HOPE."
—Hatry Grey, *Sorrow Not without Hope*

The time has come for the church that wants to reach our present and future culture in North America to focus on *spiritual reformation*. Spiritual formation, disciple making, and transformation are no longer making an impact on the culture in which we find ourselves. Rethinking, reframing, refocusing, retooling, and reforming are the frameworks for effective ministry in our twenty-first–century culture. The *re-* is critical for those who are apathetic about and disinterested in religion–the distant, dechurched, unchurched, and unsaved. They are looking for something different–something with greater impact, something with an authentic, relational, and as-you-go experience. Many are looking for restorative, redeeming, reconciling experiences that are applicable for daily life in a digital, fast-paced world. The church must explore *creating reformational experiences* rather than just religious events.

Diagnosis, treatment, and recovery demand focus, intentionality, and careful monitoring by professionals and persons stronger and wiser than the patient. When focus fades, improvement loses traction and momentum. Keeping the main thing the main thing is essential because energy is limited and must be focused on the treatment plan in order for restoration of health as quickly as possible.

Many churches, denominations, and believers focus on disciple making. Others focus on spiritual formation practices, historic rituals, and traditions. Still others are focusing on transformation principles and strategies. All of this certainly has its place and has worked to some degree when we were ministering in a church culture. However, since the early 1960s, our culture in North America has become increasingly secular, pagan, and unchurched; yet we continue to use the same strategies we used in the church culture. Jesus shifted his focus and strategies as he found himself in a variety of people groups and cultures. We need to do the same.

With fishermen, Jesus fished and enjoyed breakfast by the Sea of Galilee. With the woman at the well, he used her search for water as a pathway for communicating about the water of life. With Matthew, a tax collector, he engaged in conversations about values in life. The blind man, the Pharisees–Jesus met people on their turf and spoke to them in ways that brought a reframing and reformation to the lives they were living or the values they were holding. His presence and intentionality created teachable moments, divine appointments, and sacred places for sacred conversations that revolutionized lives, families, businesses, recreational experiences, careers, and lifestyles.

A small church grew into a medium-sized church in a college town. The church was growing numerically and in their spiritual formation practices. The programming at the church was well received by members, the membership felt cared for, and the facilities met the needs of the members. To go to the next level, the congregation engaged me as their coach to work with staff, key leaders, and entire congregation to discern where God was leading them now. We had a powerful experience rooted in their history and spiritual formation skills and passions. What happened was and is a miracle story in my estimation. Feeling led by God, this congregation had bought some apartments behind their church, thinking they would tear them down (for they were old and in need of significant repair) to make room for a church parking lot expansion. Through the coaching process, God shifted their vision and their hearts. Now the vision took on reformation characteristics as they refurbished the apartments and provided a space for intergeneration, multi-ethnic tenants. God provided the resources beyond measure, and the calling of the lay persons led them not only to rehab the apartments, but now they have bought a health care facility to care for those in need of medical care who cannot afford it. A powerful story of transformation! The tool below illustrates something of the shifts they have and are making to live into this new vision!

I always ask, when planning with churches and leading in church groups, "How can this experience bring spiritual reformation?" By now, someone is certainly saying, "What's the difference between spiritual formation and spiritual reformation?" The difference is intent, motivation, and mystery. Each distinction makes reformation possible, and is vital for the culture. Consider...

SPIRITUAL FORMATION	SPIRITUAL REFORMATION
Preserves historic traditions, sustains rituals	Creates fresh rituals and traditions to keep faith fresh
Guided by Christian calendar	Guided by daily as-you-go experiences seeking to integrate with faith
Focuses on historic spiritual practices of prayer, fasting, reflection, Scripture reading, worship	Focuses on discovering God in the midst of the moment and embracing the mystery of the unknown
About "coming to"	About "engaging with"
Informed by Scripture, reflection, prayer	Informed by mystery, community, truth, curiosity, and searching amid life
Validated by traditional metrics and values	Validated by attunement, hope, discovered truth, energy, and assurance of the presence and power of God at work
Acknowledges and creates gathering of people of faith on common journey to sustain the traditions and practices of the faith	Acknowledges, creates, and maximizes teachable moments and divine appointments in the midst of life experiences
Aligns with tradition, expectations	Attunement with Spirit; resonance with truth, hope, and health through God
Driven by elements and expectation of discipline	Driven by elements of decision, holy yearnings for pursuit of health and hope
Intent is to align and be among the faithful with history, tradition, and church practices	Intent is to discover God as the source of life; hope; and avenue to relief, restoration, and reconciliation with people and divine purpose
Often event-driven in keeping with spiritual practices, Christian calendar, baptism	Often issues from life experience driven by need for meaning, hope, and connection with divine purpose and community

Experiencing practice and sustaining of recommended spiritual practices	Experiencing aspects of faith discovering and embracing forgiveness, reconciliation, health, and direction
Creates feelings of satisfaction, faithfulness, and alignment	Creates experiences that nurture faith amid life experiences and opens next steps with God

My love for and commitment to the New Testament church's mission is reason to ask new questions. While events are helpful, they are rarely transformational, much less reformational. It is time, or past time, to consider seriously how our event-driven church culture can become experience driven in order to bring about reformation possibilities. A vacation for the soul is needed. Learning to create sacred space and place is essential if reformation as we go is a viable possibility.

Learning to ask, "What will reform the soul?" rather than, "What will people attend?" might be a starting place for rethinking, retooling, and reforming church in a twenty-first–century world. Much of the reform begins with the value system that guides the church. For instance, so many believe the primary purpose of the church is to care for the members. While this has its place, it is not the biblical mission of the church.

An example of this spiritual reformation experience is what I call "pictures that teach." Jesus was always using stories, images, and nature to teach powerful spiritual lessons. To give visibility to a spiritual truth, He took the familiar and reformed how it is seen/experienced. I invite my friends, colleagues, neighbors, and Bible study groups to use their smart-phone cameras to capture images that inform, challenge, inspire, encourage, or illuminate truths to them. We post these on our Pinterest pages and share our stories from the pictures as part of our spiritual conversations, prayers, or spiritual insights. It's fun, powerful, and spiritually reforming. This practice gives us "eyes to see and ears to hear" new images with powerful truths.

Another element of spiritual reformation involves the pastoral care value and expectations in many churches. We have to move beyond pastoral care to pastoral reformation and get back to the roots of "equipping the saints for the work of ministry" rather than the clergy being expected to do the work of ministry *for* the saints rather than *with* the saints in the pews.

The Consequences of Caring Too Much

Often the journey of recovery involves getting our focus off our pains and illness and opening up to receive support from others and often to help others. Such can often become part of the treatment and recovery as we shift from over preoccupation with our care to caring for others. Many churches are in need of recovery from spending most of their time, energy, and money just on taking care of the members rather than mobilizing members into missional experiences in and through their careers and community relationships. Shifting focus of time, energy, and resources is key to recovery. Even if only a remnant of the church shifts, it can make a significant difference in the possibility of recovery of hope.

Many congregations (districts, judicatories, associations) and pastoral leaders are crying for clear, focused pastoral leadership amid rapid change in our culture, but most are primarily getting/giving pastoral care. What's that about? What are the consequences of minimal leadership in our churches, judicatories, districts, and denominations?

THE ROOTS OF THE PASTORAL CARE MODEL IN THE CHURCH

Pastoral care is rooted in showing care through nurturing conversations, listening, giving attention during times of loss, stress, or crisis. This nurturing soft side of pastoral ministry is highly expected and highly valued by most. In fact, the care is valued more by those in the pew than by leaders. Such care has an impact on forward movement through challenge and change that most churches face today.

A congregation's high expectations lead many clergy to give most of their time and energy to caregiving rather than to leadership. If the clergy are not attentive in times of stress and crisis, members feel ignored, devalued, or disliked. This hurts relationships, damages congregational culture, and inhibits leadership.

Another root of pastoral care is that many, if not most, pastors are far more skilled and comfortable with their caregiving skills than their leadership skills. For most trained in seminaries prior to 1990, pastoral care was highlighted as the epitome of a good pastor. Those trained most recently are at least introduced to the value of leadership, but unfortunately, in far too many cases, the introduction is so elementary that those pastors face their first churches with fear and limited training.

Most churches and other denominational organizations get stuck or become irrelevant and out of touch when pastoral care concerns and skills override leadership concerns and skills. Caring is a needed and important function. However, when pastoral care is overdone and overexpected, a church becomes ingrown, maintenance-minded, and often sacrifices the biblical mandate/mission for being a loving/nurturing church. I am certainly not advocating that pastors/churches should stop caring. *I am* pleading *for a reallocation of time/energy/resources and expectations to give a new, more forward-looking balance than an inward-looking/caring focus.*

7

What Is Distinctive about Missional Leadership?

"WHILE THERE IS LIFE THERE IS HOPE—
AND WHILE THERE IS HOPE THERE IS LIFE."
—E. E. Holmes, *Joyful through Hope*

Any group needs people to lead the way. Who are those who legitimize and model the new in your ministry setting? Their impact will become visible when those of vision and passion share and celebrate the movement of God with their friends, families, colleagues, and community. Celebration is key and intentional, but unfortunately is often overlooked and taken for granted. When a church ignores celebration, leaders are demotivated, discouraged, and often become disillusioned. When the stories of ministry by passionate people come forth, vision grows and touches new persons. They become new leaders. Communities are impacted and transformed. and the gift of faith matures while the church is energized and renewed. In short, leader fulfillment comes when leaders are empowered, supported, and encouraged to follow their calling and passion to live missional lives of service.

The chart in chapter 5, "What Is Distinctive about Missional Leadership?" introduced this concept. Defining these aspects brought clarity for me. Go back and look at the chart again. It gives a snapshot of what leaders and churches value and support.

The key here is to move from shifting internal values to practical solutions to nurture dreams, callings, and gifting.

How Pastoral Care
Can Be Disciple Shaping
(Moving Forward in Faith through Caregiving)

Pastoral care can have a disciple-shaping impact when we pay close attention to the movement of the Spirit and the hunger of the person visited. Moving forward to pastoral reformation deepens impact and relevancy. Such insight and experience hold a freshness for me and add a greater dimension of disciple making among individuals and through the pastoral care expected by most congregations and practiced by many clergy and lay leaders.w

Most congregations expect consistent, genuine, skillful pastoral care of those in their congregation facing crisis situations: illness, bereavement, domestic struggles, economic challenges, job or status loss, faith issues, or career decisions. Many pastors are gifted and called to such a shepherding, nurturing, caregiving ministry. Other pastors are not as gifted or called to such care. They may well be more equipped for the preaching/teaching ministry or skilled at administration or evangelism. Some pastors work most creatively connecting the local parish to other congregations or institutions. They build partnerships in the community as advocates for the poor, jobless, homeless, and those treated unjustly. Still other pastors have a deep passion and calling for disciple making built around spiritual formation, Bible study, prayer, and fulfilling the Great Commission and the Great Commandment through mentoring and multiplying ministry by the "equipping of the saints for the work of ministry" (Eph. 4:11–12).

The tension and struggle for clergy to fulfill their calling and gifting while meeting the expectations of congregations for pastoral care is a balancing act at best. At worst this dance often drains the energy of the clergy and congregation because of a mismatch of calling and expectations. Many, if not most, clergy and congregations do not spend enough time exploring and finding their best match. They set everyone up for disappointments, struggles, and persistent tensions.

How can pastoral care be reformed as a disciple-making part of ministry rather than just a caregiving ministry of presence? Caregiving is more than holding hands, offering prayers, and being a calming presence. Disciple-shaping caregiving is about helping those visited find and take next steps in their faith formation—through improving their understanding of who God is and how God works, along with exploring together in community the question: What is God teaching us now?

I had this epiphany recently as I visited my dying aunt. This spiritually rich and memorable experience put a deep mark in each of our lives, offering hope, healing, and a new awareness of how God moves. My aunt and I have always been close. We have enjoyed many spiritual and church conversations, joining our hands and hearts in prayer; but that day was different. Assuming my nephew pastor role, I inquired, "How are you doing today?" I kissed her on the forehead as she lay in her nursing-home bed. She grabbed my hand, squeezing it as tight as she could, smiled, and declared, "It's so good to see you! Thanks for coming to see me! I love you!"

Her weak but strong grip on my hand indicated she was weaker than the last time we had visited. We didn't talk for maybe three or four minutes, just holding hands and looking deeply into each other's eyes. I saw something different, but I had seen that look before. Something was on her heart. I asked, "Would you like for me to get a chair and just sit beside your bed for a while?"

"Yes, would you?" she whispered, and she sustained her grip on my hand. I found myself praying in my spirit, "Lord what's going on here? Help me pay close attention and be who you and she need me to be during this visit!"

We just sat there, holding hands, occasionally easing into a deeper place in the conversation. I gently asked, "What's going on with you today? Would you like to talk about something?" No sooner had I asked than I noticed a big tear come into her weakening eyes, but her grip remained firm.

She eased into conversations about her concern for herself, her family, her grandchildren. Her memory faded into confused talk (part of dementia), but I waited and kept my prayerful focus. I asked, "Anything else?" She pondered and worked hard to recapture the moment, and I prayed the Spirit might give her peace and me patience and discernment. The conversation continued for about ten minutes as we cried together. I offered her words of comfort, understanding, and the assurance that God was in the room and in our hearts. He understood her longings and feelings. She gripped my hand harder and looked clearly into my eyes and declared with great confidence, "I know God understands. I needed to know that you understand too!" Those intimate moments gave us a new understanding of each other, the issues at the forefront of life, and a fresh awareness of God's presence, comfort, and understanding of life's challenges. What a great gift! We will always remember that moment and be deeply grateful for the assurance that God knows more than we do and that we must trust Him and one another.

I truly believe that each of us moved forward and went deeper in our spiritual formation because of that pastoral care moment. The learnings continue for me even as I write this. I will continue to journal and reflect on those powerful moments where we nurtured each other as we experienced God nurturing us individually and together!

LESSONS LEARNED INCLUDE

1. Pastoral care can facilitate disciple shaping and deepen spiritual formation and reformation for those cared for and for the caregiver.
2. Disciple shaping and reformation is a needed and often absent or unacknowledged function of a disciple-making ministry.
3. Being in the moment and paying attention to the one needing care is important.
4. Even more important for all concerned are our keen awareness and acknowledging of God's care and understanding in that moment. There, through pastoral care occasions, we discover spiritual formation possibilities.
5. When disciple shaping happens, the Spirit changes both the visitor and the visited in ways that transform the heart and the head and give assurance of the presence and power of God at work.
6. The power of touch is a deep communication for those who have little or no voice.
7. Creating a sacred space and place nurtures the spiritual growth possibilities for all.
8. Further prayer and reflection deepen the impact and nurture the spiritual awareness and formation of the divine appointment and teachable moment.

Trying to keep up with everything going on in some churches is exhausting. God's people, both ministers and congregation, ought not be exhausted from doing church. Many churches have tried to fix perceived problems by adding programs, believing that adding one more thing will meet more needs, engage more people, and provide more opportunities. In reality, the same staff and congregational leaders step up and take on more. If this describes your church and you want to simplify and discover new ways to move your church forward, you may be ready to consider a coach approach.

8

Moving from Maintenance to Missional to Incarnational Engagement

BEYOND COMFORTABLE LEADERSHIP: THE PRICE OF UNSTICKING STUCK CHURCHES

"THOSE THAT HOPE LITTLE CANNOT GROW MUCH."
—George MacDonald, *The Hope of the Gospel*

Moving from a weakened and ill state to health demands doing things differently and following professional counsel. Such often moves patients beyond their comfort zones. Many days after surgery a therapist asked me to make moves that were painful and uncomfortable but were essential for me to regain strength and stamina and to prevent pneumonia. The doctors knew best. I followed their recommendations. Often it involved pain, discomfort, and stretching beyond my preferences in order for my health to be restored and for progress to be made!

Many organizations, people, and churches are stuck these days. *Stuck* means living in created places, values, and beliefs that make us feel secure. *Stuck* is about being primarily inward focused and narcissistic in concerns, use of resources, and attention. In churches *stuck* is probable after cycling programming and practices to preserve rather than impact. Being stuck also suggests using a larger percentage of time and energy concerned more about those already connected to the church rather than those beyond membership and walls. Stuck also emerges when leaders and churches are hesitant to take risks due to the fear of disappointing or agitating their base.

As I write this, we are seeing this in the stalemate in our government. Neither political group wants to solve problems for fear of losing their base and possibly their jobs. Unfortunately, or fortunately, deadlines are around the corner. These politicians seem to be willing to jeopardize the financial stability of our country just to preserve their identity and their jobs. How scary and sad.

Finally, *leaders and churches that are stuck most often choose to be stuck.* They choose to stay in their comfort zones, living in and with the familiar that creates a safe and secure spot. Many churches face this same stalemate—finances and membership decline, apathy grows in the pew and pulpit, and the church has less and less influence in the community. The only problem is that living safe and secure works for the short term, but for long term it often leads to apathy, diminishing commitment, atrophy of needed muscles, isolation, and insulation that typically lead to dysfunction and death.

Let me be quick to say, I understand wanting to feel secure and safe, take few risks, and desire to preserve peace and often a job! Been there on several occasions. Certainly no one wants to be seen as a troublemaker or as someone who stirs up trouble just for trouble's sake. In tough economic times, who wants to risk losing a job! The issue here is one of impact, influence, and effectiveness. *Do you want to be a leader of a church with impact, influence, and effectiveness or to be seen as in a church that is safe, secure, and insulated from others?* How does that line up with the mandate for believers and churches found in the Great Commission? The Christian message is all about being people of faith (Heb. 11), willing to go to a place we do not know (Gen. 12), and putting our hand to the plow and not looking back (Lk. 17).

Scripture is replete with commands to "fear not" (more than 170 times)! Yet believers, leaders, and churches choose to stay safe, secure, and take few risks—certainly not risks that are so uncalculated that we must call upon faith, a faith that is dead without works (Jas. 1).

I can hear some say, "This guy is calling us to be reckless!" Seems to me that this is exactly the challenge from Christ, who broke all kind of stereotypes and barriers, and pushed through fears on every hand so that others might know! I also know we are not Christ!

What keeps leaders and churches stuck? The core of this might be found in three human emotions that challenge us—sense of loss, fear, and desire for comfort. These three basic emotions manifest themselves in such powerful ways in lives, families, classes, churches, and even denominations that we choose safe and secure over fulfillment, obedience, faith, risks, and effectiveness. Our motto often becomes "Safe at all costs," while Christ calls us to take up our cross daily and follow him. He even told us it would be lonely, difficult, and risky, like being sheep among wolves (Lk. 10).

Consider the chart below and do some self-assessment reflecting on your patterns of behavior (as leader and church) and what often guides and dictates your reaction to moving from comfort to challenge, from safety to success, from fear to fulfillment. What paralyzes you? What keeps you living in comfort and could be keeping you from greater success and fulfillment and from being more aligned with Christ's calling on your life/church?

Challenges That Keep Churches Stuck
(How Challenges Often Manifest Themselves)

Loss	Fear	Comfort
Of identity in church and community	Of being seen as unfaithful to tradition	Needing stability in a world filled with change
Of position/status in church if it grows	Of the unknown—new standards/strategies	Knowing and trusting protocol, procedures, and policies
Of personal preferences in style, music, worship, Bible, hymnals	Of displeasing God and our history and founders	With beliefs in the "God I know"
Of family or community respect	Of what others might say	With traditional programming, buildings
Of hymnal, organ, choirs	Of technology, worship teams, and instruments	With familiarity of music style, message, and delivery
Of comfort zone with lyrics, translations	Of having to learn new lyrics, styles	With verbal messages in a visual world
Of permission to rest in our safe, comfortable sanctuaries removed from the uncomfortable world	Of being called to be people of faith who risk and stretch into God's call	With things as they are and seeing no need to change. "It's good enough for me!"

Finding the Yes That Moves You Forward

Often churches seeking to upgrade or reboot themselves to improve effectiveness run into a stalemate. Pockets of resistance almost inevitably emerge. This is where the coach approach takes on deeper roots and more value as a service. The coach watches and listens deeply for what is going on in the conversation—sometimes observing and listening to that which is not voiced but is evident. This is where the coach's prayer life is critical as part of the preparation for a congregational coaching experience.

The coach works to clarify what is really going on in a given situation. Usually it is emotionally charged. Quite often coaching conversations become personal. Typically such situations revolve around personal preferences and comfort areas or tradition tied to families or personalities. Getting clear about these connections and realities can be challenging. Such clarity can also bring immediate relief if connections are discovered or discerned rather than declared. Honesty in a congregation often releases and fuels hope. If the group works, using some of the tools offered here, and still misses clarity and understanding about their situation, the coach can ask permission to share what this trained, experienced outsider is seeing. If the group allows, the coach can then label what he/she sees and check it out with the group. Sometimes a "eureka moment" erupts for the group. Other times the group chooses to deny, avoid, or resist. Then the coach must let them suffer the consequences of their own decisions.

The coach then has to be nonjudgmental and remain unattached to the outcome, allowing the "stuck" church to follow their own decisions and remain stuck. I often find myself wondering when churches will learn that their fate is often determined by the decisions they make (or, in some cases, do not make).

I have found this exercise to be helpful. On newsprint, write in random order words such as:

Fear	Faith	Fact
Feeling	Alignment	Attunement
Agreement	Collaboration	Consensus
Unity	Uniformity	Judgment
Support		

Ask the group to act prayerfully and personally. After a few moments, arrange them in small groups around tables. Ask them to identify what is driving their disagreement or discomfort. Let them each write personal issues down on one side of a three-by-five-inch card. Then on the other side of the card instruct them each to write the issue that is driving the congregational discomfort or disagreement. Invite them to share with their small table group their discoveries. Then the coach takes a collective recording from the large group and keeps a running tally on newsprint for the group to see. The coach then asks the group, "What does this group tally say about you? your church?"

Often this exercise tends to surface (directly or indirectly) the presence of a church bully or two or three. Bullies often keep churches stuck by their fears of hurting the feelings of the bully, or of losing the finances or family of the bully. Sometimes such is not a founded fear. Other times it reveals something the congregational coach needs to work with to get clarity, focus, and direction from the group. Facing and dealing with church bullies opens many locked paths to hope for the future of a church. Until the congregation deals with bullies, the church stays stuck, deepens unhealthy patterns, and hides the lies that bind them from the freedom of the call of Christ.

Another framework is found in the following handout. I typically review with pastor/staff and key leaders some powerful challenges and coaching questions for helping churches in and moving through transition. We use the Funnel of Church Ministry Engagement on page 45 as a focusing element for further self-assessment.

COACHING QUESTIONS TO CONSIDER

Using the funnel...

1. Where are you now?
2. Where is your church now?
3. What percentage of your resources go to each ministry area? *(time, energy, money, leaders)*
4. Where is God leading you now? What might you need to do?
5. What is needed to deepen your impact and influence?
6. What will the church look like as deeper engagement happens?

Once they identify where they sense they are as leaders and congregation, then we explore the following guide for leading a church in and through transition to gain further clarity, direction, and hope.

Leading Churches in and through Transition

PREVALENT LEADERSHIP ISSUES

Intentional Prayerful Preparation/Discernment
- Collaboration
- Focused, intentional prayer
- Journaling
- Peer support

Funnel of Church Ministry Engagement

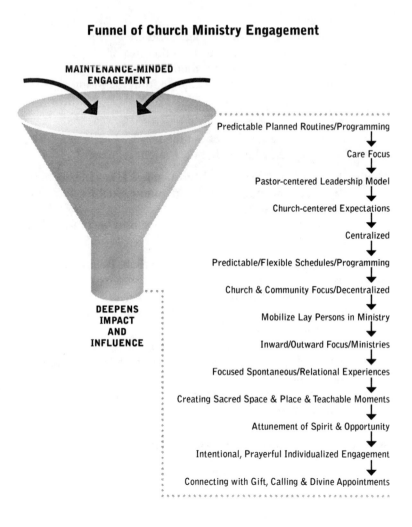

MAINTENANCE-MINDED
ENGAGEMENT

Predictable Planned Routines/Programming
↓
Care Focus
↓
Pastor-centered Leadership Model
↓
Church-centered Expectations
↓
Centralized
↓
Predictable/Flexible Schedules/Programming
↓
Church & Community Focus/Decentralized
↓
Mobilize Lay Persons in Ministry
↓
Inward/Outward Focus/Ministries
↓
Focused Spontaneous/Relational Experiences
↓
Creating Sacred Space & Place & Teachable Moments
↓
Attunement of Spirit & Opportunity
↓
Intentional, Prayerful Individualized Engagement
↓
Connecting with Gift, Calling & Divine Appointments

DEEPENS
IMPACT
AND
INFLUENCE

Self-Awareness–Questions to Ask Yourself
- What pushes your buttons?
- What/who are you willing to lose to let your church become what you are praying for?
- How much ownership for new ideas is present in the group/church?
- What are the consequences when the new becomes reality?
- What is the degree of trust/distrust of you/among members?

Identifying Fears
- How can you identify the fears and the fearful?
- What would minimize/address their fears?
- How can you/others help them?
- How can you lead/create change from the inside out?

Identifying Change Agents/Remnant
- Who are the advocates for the new?
- What do they see/feel about the new?
- Whom do they know that they might influence?

Getting Clear about What Can/Must Change (Tangible/Concrete)
- What are the negotiables and nonnegotiables for church leaders/for pastor?
- What must change in the church for it to become a church of hope?

Getting Clear about What Is in Transition (Soft, Relational, Emotional)
- Who will resist the new?
- What are they losing, or what do they fear losing because of the proposed change?
- How can those fears be acknowledged/heard/addressed?
- What is the degree of stress/tension that indicates reassessment is needed?
- Does the stress come from real possibilities or from unfounded fears?

POSSIBLE LEADERSHIP SOLUTIONS/TIPS

"Observe All Things"–Pay Attention (Mt. 28:20)

Listen More Than Talk

Ask More Than Declare

Count the Cost Before...

Explore with Advocates, Legitimizers, and Core Resisters:
- Benefits
- Challenges
- Opportunities
- Change from inside out rather than outside in
- Generational preferences/perspectives
- Consequences if...
- How others have dealt with the same issue(s)
- What did they learn?

Learn to Negotiate Yes
- What is needed and by whom?
- What are the win-win possibilities?
- What are we all willing to gain?
- What are we all willing to lose?
- What will be the power of yes for others?
- What will be the impact/power of no for others?

Maximize the Learning from the Decision(s)
- Drill down (bring to a clearer focus)
- Explore benefits/consequences
- How does our decision align with our mission?
- How does our decision align with or is a disconnect from our divine mission as a church?

My book *Making Shifts without Making Waves* also offers some practical coaching skills and models for leaders working with churches in transitions.

Resources to Consider

Bridges, William. *Transitions: Making Sense of Life's Changes.* Cambridge, Mass.: Da Capo Press, 2004.

Cialdini, Robert. *Influence: The Psychology of Persuasion.* New York: Morrow, 1993.

Cloud, Henry. *Necessary Endings: The Employees, Businesses, and Relationships That All of Us Have to Give Up in Order to Move Forward.* New York: HarperBusiness, 2011.

Deutschman, Alan. *Change or Die: The Three Keys to Change at Work and in Life.* New York: HarperBusiness, 2007.

Hammett, Edward, and James Pierce. *Making Shifts without Making Waves: A Coach Approach to Soulful Leadership.* Saint Louis: Chalice Press, 2009.

Hauck, Wally. *The Art of Leading: 3 Principles for Predictable Performance Improvement.* Milford, Conn.: Optimum Leadership, 2010.

Ricci, Ron, and Carl Wiese. *The Collaboration Imperative: Executive Strategies for Unlocking Your Organization's True Potential.* San Jose: Cisco, 2011.

Vander Meer, Lew. *Recovering from Churchism.* Grand Rapids, Mich.: Edenridge Press, 2011.

Yohannan, K. P. *Revolution in World Missions: One Man's Journey to Change a Generation.* Carrollton, Tex.: GFA Books, 2009.

9

Bullying in the Church and What to Do about It

"HOPE BEGINS IN THE DARK,
THE STUBBORN HOPE THAT IF YOU JUST SHOW UP
AND TRY TO DO THE RIGHT THING,
THE DAWN WILL COME."
—Anne Lamott, *Bird by Bird*

Recovery has a lot to do with a good attitude, consistency of healthy support systems, and a desire to make progress. Those who were most helpful in my physical recovery had great attitudes, offered realistic and attainable goals, and were consistent in their prayer support and appropriate presence and encouragement. I did have a few caregivers, therapists, and physicians who were pushy, ill-tempered, and more concerned about their schedules than my understanding and progress. They did not help my recovery. I felt as if I were being bullied by them, and interacting with them was not helpful for me.

Bullying is a growing issue in our culture–in schools, businesses, organizations, families, and communities. It starts early in life. A six-year-old got to take two cookies to school lunch on her birthday. That afternoon, Dad asked her if she enjoyed the cookies he had placed as a surprise in her lunch bag.

"Well, I enjoyed one. Loretta ate the other one."

"How did Loretta get your cookie?" Dad inquired.

"She made me give it to her. She said she would stop being my friend if I did not give her a cookie."

Bullying has leaped ahead as a major problem in churches and other religious organizations, and not just with children. It often hides in the shadows of being correct, staying politically right, gaining control/power, or insisting this is the way I/we like it done or tradition shows us the way it has always been done.

Church bullies are growing across the country as churches struggle with decline in numbers—attendance, membership, participation, impact, finances, and loyalty issues. Often church bullies surface and target the pastor and staff, blaming and often falsely accusing their leaders for the decline in their church's metrics or status. While certainly leaders do bear some of the responsibility, more often than not these diminishing numbers and lessening impact come from pulpit, pew, and cultural issues.

How does a pastor, staff, and congregation deal with church bullies who surface and practice pastor bashing[1] as they work to get their way? This presents a tense and fine line for many of my clergy coaching clients these days.

How to Recognize Bullying in the Church

Change is a dirty word for many churches, and many churches and clergy have little or no training or experience in dealing with the exponential change we find ourselves amidst these days. Such a deficit raises fears, anxieties, and frustration levels when things do not go a preferred or familiar way in a church.

Having coached several thousand hours with clergy and other church leaders, I am certain pastor bashing and bullying is a critical issue in many churches—regardless of size, type, theology, age of church, or median age of the congregation. Church bullies not only do not want to change their preferences, but they want to blame others and often falsely accuse in order to protect their preferred ways or comfort zone. I have heard of or experienced church bullying in a variety of ways/places in a church:

- A Bible study group of older adults repeatedly attack the pastor and staff with unjust, brutal, judgmental words accompanied by a spirit of anger, revenge, or desire for their way.
- A finance or stewardship committee holds the church purse strings as if the money were in their household family budget. They often control what is or is not permitted by controlling the spending based on their personal preferences rather than the church's mission or desires.

- An active, engaged lay leader has his or her hand in everything not just to help but also to exercise some control in the way things are done to ensure his/her preferences are not ignored by others.
- Youth parents or guardians become the mouthpiece for their child or grandchild in order to exercise control by evaluating all others by their personal preferences of parenting styles, disciplinary actions, dress preferences, programming preferences, and standards. These parents usually are demanding, vindictive, persevering, and filled with anger and a desire for revenge.
- A deacon body or trustee group is more committed to their personal preferences or comfort zones than to the divine mission for the church. This control is most often exercised in micro-managing pastor and staff, wanting the pastor to be all things to all people while keeping everyone happy. The mission of the church becomes maintenance—by the deacons' or trustees' standards—and often inhibits pastors from living into Christ's call in their lives and the church.
- Clergy bullies are driven by personal preferences, comfort zones, and often seek to force the church into molds or styles they are professionally more comfortable with rather than contextualizing ministry and facing their own learning curves and challenges.

Bullies in church are often recognizable. They demonstrate hunger for power and control, maintaining their preferences regardless of anyone else's needs. It's all about them, their values, their preferences, and their comfort—with little if any desire to align to the corporate mission and vision much less a biblical mandate.

Managing Church Bullies and Minimizing Their Impact

Church bullies like to stir up trouble; they love attention about as much as they like getting their way. The more attention you give them, the more they stir the pot. Of course, when you don't give them attention, it escalates their anger, determination, and vengeance. Often bullies cannot let go of their agenda. It has them at the heart, and no one sees a situation as they do! They truly believe they are doing the right thing and are saving their church. However, more often than not, they have tunnel vision, so their way is the only way.

If the church or group plays into their game, the bully wins; and often the pastor, staff, and/or church loses because the community learns about the fight at *that* church. Bullies create a bad reputation for the church, and often people weary of the internal war and conflict leave the church because of the bully's control rather than the issue the bully is mad about. A group of bullies can destroy a church by their determination to get their way or sway people to their side. They often really do not care about the pastor, church, community reputation, or wounds they inflict. It's all about *their* agenda!

So how do you manage dealing with bullies within a Christian context? How do you deal with such vengeance, anger, self-centeredness, and hurt in a redemptive and Christian manner? That is the million-dollar question for so many, and many pastors and churches have weakened because they opt to do nothing, wanting to avoid hurting anyone. The truth is, the church is allowing one or two, or a small group, to hurt if not kill the spirit and mission of their church to preserve someone's feelings. How long will a church let the desires of a few condemn or control the future of their church?

Some Tips Learned from My Coaching Clients and Personal Experiences

- Be prayerful and intentional as the situation and understanding of personalities involved are discerned. Follow principles in Matthew 18.
- Invite a neutral outsider to help with the process so decision making is clear and the bully does not feel an insider has his or her own agenda.
- The issue has to be dealt with by the trusted lay leaders who have earned the right to talk and be heard and are willing to step up to the challenge of leadership.
- The clergy are the target and need to enlist and empower the lay leaders to determine next steps and carry out the desires of the congregation.
- Go to the bully and face him/her with perceptions and realities. Give focused opportunity for lay leaders, pastors, and staff, if appropriate, to respond to issues, asking, "What do you need from me that you are not getting now?" Following this encounter, negotiate with lay leaders and the congregation if their demands are in line with the congregation's mission.

- Invite trusted friends and colleagues of the disgruntled bully to become advocates for further conversation, but be careful not to get triangulated in the relationship.
- Scripture offers some support. If these ideas do not work, then you take the conflict to the congregation. This can be done in some church governance, but, depending on a possible pathology of the bully, it could become detrimental and destroy, or certainly scar deeply, those involved as well as the reputation of the congregation in the community at large.

Alan Deutschman, in his book *Change or Die,* points out that there are effective and ineffective ways of introducing and managing change in any organization. Typically the three Fs are practiced by most bullies in the church.

THE THREE Fs—INEFFECTIVE WAYS TO DEAL WITH BULLIES

FACTS: which assumes people will deal with issues rationally. Bullies force FACTS, quoting scripture and/or tradition and declaring this is the way it is! This approach rarely generates effective change. Facts really do not matter to most—it's their feelings that matter most!

FEARS: that would appeal to emotions. Generally, many facing change go to their fears of losing things such as their familiarity or comfort in the present situation. Bullies will make threats and stir emotions of distrust, disrespect, and anger to preserve their comfort zones. This is reviewed eloquently by Gordon MacDonald in *Who Stole My Church?*[2]

FORCE: that is about falling back on the moral authority of your positions. Bullies declare, "We have never done it that way before and we are not going to start now!" They often create and circulate petitions, withhold their tithes and participation and enlist their inactive friends to vote to keep things the way they prefer.[3]

How often do these Fs show up in the way you or your church responds to, introduces, or manages change? How did that work for you? What were the consequences?

THE THREE Rs—EFFECTIVE WAYS TO DEAL WITH BULLIES

More often than not bullies do not choose to practice these effective tools. They resort to the ineffective means of derailing or sabotaging change by practicing the three Fs and avoiding these three Rs at all cost. The three Rs provide a possible roadmap for minimizing and maybe diffusing the impact of bullies.

RELATE: speaks of building authentic emotional relationships with the individual or groups involved. Spending time in dialogue with those the bullies are against is often avoided or resisted by bullies. How can the accused/bullied and the bullies work on this together? What might it look like for each?

REPEAT: In dealing with change we need to learn to do many little things differently. Repeating the new is a way of building familiarity off of the new desire. When we change the behaviors, the feelings do follow as repetition builds familiarity. In all likelihood, the bully and the bullied will need to learn and practice some new attitudes and behaviors to find common ground. What would this look like in your setting?

REFRAME: is about changing from the inside out rather than the outside in. This reframing hinges on relationships, sharing each other's life stories and the reason they have certain preferences and what make life meaningful to them.[4]

Such creates greater understanding and often leads to *Making Shifts Without Making Waves.* How might this be practiced in your context? The *Making Shifts* book provides coaching models to guide individuals and groups to a point of common ground and mutual respect and understanding.[5]

Whether in school, communities, families, or churches, bullies must be dealt with lest the poison they spew negatively impacts forward movement, generates polarization, and fuels a detrimental reputation in the community. How might bullies be silenced or at least minimized and the membership become more empowered to move the church forward?

Silencing Church Bullies
While Empowering Church Members

Church bullies are in most every church working to achieve or retain their power, control, influence. Some are more visible and vocal than others. More often than not they emerge not as bullies but as people with strong convictions about the way things need to be done in their church. They may want to preserve family or church traditions. They may believe, since they are charter members or significant givers to the church budget or projects, that they deserve a stronger voice than others. If and when there is some pushback from others, often the person of conviction turns into a church bully determined to get *his/her* way! Such behavior frequently consumes massive amounts of time, energy, and sometimes resources from pastor, staff, and/or deacons/elders, the session, presbytery, district superintendent, and the congregation.

Bullies often become a major distraction from the biblical mission of the church. Bullies are more concerned about their agenda and mission than God's mission. Or, in some cases, they are genuinely convinced their mission as a bully is blessed by God and that their behavior is a way of showing faithfulness to what they believe is God's desire for *their* church.

As a congregational coach and consultant for twenty-five plus years, and having been on church staffs for twenty years, I have met, seen, heard about, and engaged many church bullies! The challenge is how to silence or effectively deal with church bullies while empowering members who often sit down and let the bully have his or her way in order to keep peace in the family or the church family and community.

Ask, Don't Tell—the Pathway to Resolution

As I have personally and professionally encountered church bullies over the decades, I have learned that telling off or proclaiming to the bully is like pouring gasoline on a fire! A telling posture only intensifies the bully's determination. Conflict emerges, polarization appears, and the next thing you know the pastor and staff are often the scapegoats, or at least the ones that get burned or consumed by the debates. Such intensity drains energy, distracts from the church mission, and often breeds a deep discouragement, if not depression, among key church leaders.

I confess I have known church bullies up close! I, like some of you, have such bullies in my extended family circle. I know the heartache, stress, and dissension such realities create within family systems and not just in local congregations. The pain is real. The challenges are deep and wide. The distrust and lack of respect grows and calls forth a genuine need for forgiveness, reconciliation, recovering hope, and healing.

In professional and personal settings, I finally discovered that if I simply ask powerful coaching questions, use appropriate humor, and learn and practice self-management, some headway can be made and at least a focus can be found to work on, rather than all efforts leading to an unfortunate, destructive outcome. I learned early to ask rather than to tell. Over the decades I have learned more coaching skills and refined skills of self-management, nonattachment, and nonjudgment, giving up my agenda to help others clarify their agenda issues. I am not suggesting this has been easy or fun, but I have found the coach approach to be a powerful tool in dealing effectively with church bullies and in empowering the congregation to move forward. The joy is to create a safe and sacred space for a congregational or group coaching experience.

Framing the time together and agreeing on desired outcomes is essential. Once a covenant is mutually built and agreed upon, we launch into a coaching experience that includes the following:

- A clear set of desired outcomes
- A mutually agreed-upon time frame
- A set of ground rules for the coaching experience
- A safe and sacred place to explore together options and what a win-win might look like
- Use of appropriate and well-timed humor to release the tension but also to provide reflective opportunity
- A skilled and committed coach who has bathed the experience in prayer and thoughtful discernment and is willing to be a neutral coach in the experience
- A coach willing to stand up to the bully if needed
- A coach committed to checking out a variety of perceptions, realities, or false realities with the larger group and trusting the Spirit and the group to gain a deeper understanding and engagement

Nonnegotiables for the Coach

The key, if there is one, to this coach approach is the self-management discernment, humor, and courage of the coach. The clarity of desired outcomes by the group is crucial. The coach must always be careful...

- Not to make dismantling the bully the primary focus, but rather hear out the group and give everyone an equal voice in the process
- To be forward focused in desired outcomes of the coaching process
- To withhold personal judgment or opinion, instead following the group's energy and the Spirit's leadership
- To be in the moment—not with a planned strategy of silencing someone. This must be guided by the Spirit in the conversation. If it is planned, it leads to revenge or fuels hatred, and that is not the role of church.
- To be discerning, clear, concise, and always checking perceptions with the group through questions such as: (1) What do you make of this response? (2) How does the group's response inform your position/opinions? (3) How will you respond now? (4) What do you need from this group in light of this discussion?
- To trust the group/congregation to find and work toward a win-win collaborative solution

Watching the Process Move People Forward

In congregational coaching experiences, I have watched the Spirit of God and the spirit of the congregation silence (or reduce the influence) of their bullies and mobilize their members. I observed a bully being voted down in a coaching session. The bully had a real issue with some lights that had been installed in the fellowship hall to facilitate contemporary worship. The bully stood in our gathering and took issue with this and claimed the church never approved the purchase or installation of these lights. I asked, as coach, "How many in this room of 200 people agree with what she just said?" No one raised a hand to defend her position. I then asked the bully, "What does that say to you?" She sat down, and, eventually, left the church.

It is a powerful teacher for all present. An insider of the congregation cannot do this without high risk of pushback and explosive personalized consequences. An outsider who is a well-trained coach still has risks, but they are not as volatile or severe. An outsider does not "have a dog in the fight" or a personal attachment to the person, church, or issues.

Through congregational coaching experiences, I have seen:

- A church bully whose political issues of church and state, Christian and national, flags surfaced in a congregational coaching session as a point of contention. The coach, knowing nothing of the history of this person or the issue, was able to check it out with the larger group, and no one else in the room acknowledged they shared the bully's opinion. The coach simply asked, "'What does this say to you? to the group?" After those present did not speak up for her position on this issue, the bully declared, "I guess I got my answer." She sat down and hasn't spoken up about the issue again in several years.

- A church bully with issues over constitutionality of some actions by the church and the church's "lack of attention to *Robert's Rules of Order*" had dominated countless business sessions, deacon meetings, and staff meetings making his point! His constant arguments had wearied everyone and kept the church from moving forward. The outside coach was able to hear him out, ask some powerful questions that heightened his understanding, explored options with him, and then in large group setting checked it out with the group. The bully did not go away, but he certainly calmed

down and allowed and even encouraged other ideas to surface and take root in the church. His actions, as a result of
coaching, empowered others to move forward!
• Another bully wanted her (could have just as easily been
a male bully) way with the color of carpet in the sanctu-
ary; another wanted her way with the color of walls in the
church. In another situation it was people wanting their way
about the use of screens and visual aids in the worship setting. Regardless of the issue, when a person or group of
persons rally for "their way," bullies are being birthed.

Church bullies can be male or female, young or old, of different
ethnicities or cultural groups, rich or poor, with rural or urban or
suburban roots, long-term or recent new members, or even guests.
Often a church culture of love and a desire to avoid conflict creates
a perfect environment for bullies to emerge and try to dominate
decision making. Once longtime, valued (for whatever reason),
members surface with a dominating opinion, the church often en-
ables the bullies to act out, and the congregation gives them power
to get their way. This response is often born of fear of disrupting
the fellowship of the church. At other times it is out of respect for
the individual or his/her family. Or members, in attempting to be
tolerant, declare, "That's just the way he/she is."

Bullies cannot dominate unless the leaders and the congregation enable it. The risks in calling out or confronting the bully are
high, and often the price to pay is severe. Such is the reason a
guided/coached congregational process can naturally function to
help label issues, clarify challenges, and often minimize the impact
of the bully and empower the congregation to move forward.

Resources to Consider

Greenfield, Guy. *The Wounded Minister: Healing from and Preventing
Personal Attacks.* Grand Rapids, Mich.: Baker Books, 2001.
Haugk, Kenneth. *Antagonists in the Church: How to Identify and Deal
with Destructive Conflict.* Minneapolis: Augsburg, 1988.
McIntosh, Gary. *It Only Hurts on Monday: Why Pastors Quit and What
You Can Do about It.* Saint Charles, Ill.: Churchsmart Resources,
1998.
Orlowski, Barbara M. www.churchexiters.com.
_____. *Spiritual Abuse Recovery: Dynamic Research on Finding a
Place of Wholeness.* Eugene, Oreg.: Wipf and Stock, 2010.
VanVonderan, Jeff. www.spiritualabuse.com.

PART III

Living into Hope in Your Church

explores...

- When Change Is Needed but Not Wanted
- The Power of Congregational Coaching
- New Dance Steps in Ministry
- When Leaders Change, Churches Change
- Culture, Not Numbers, Matters Now
- Creating Hope Builders in Your Church

The Old Way Has to Go

I insist—and God backs me up on this—that there be no going along with the crowd, the empty-headed, mindless crowd. They've refused for so long to deal with God that they've lost touch not only with God but with reality itself. They can't think straight anymore. Feeling no pain, they let themselves go in sexual obsession, addicted to every sort of perversion.

But that's no life for you. You learned Christ! My assumption is that you have paid careful attention to him, been well instructed in the truth precisely as we have it in Jesus. Since, then, we do not have the excuse of ignorance, everything—and I do mean everything—connected with that old way of life has to go. It's rotten through and through. Get rid of it! And then take on an entirely new way of life—a God-fashioned life, a life renewed from the inside and working itself into your conduct as God accurately reproduces his character in you.

What this adds up to, then, is this: no more lies, no more pretense. Tell your neighbor the truth. In Christ's body we're all connected to each other, after all. When you lie to others, you end up lying to yourself.

Go ahead and be angry. You do well to be angry—but don't use your anger as fuel for revenge. And don't stay angry. Don't go to bed angry. Don't give the Devil that kind of foothold in your life.

Did you used to make ends meet by stealing? Well, no more! Get an honest job so that you can help others who can't work.

Watch the way you talk. Let nothing foul or dirty come out of your mouth. Say only what helps, each word a gift.

Don't grieve God. Don't break his heart. His Holy Spirit, moving and breathing in you, is the most intimate part of your life, making you fit for himself. Don't take such a gift for granted.

Make a clean break with all cutting, backbiting, profane talk. Be gentle with one another, sensitive. Forgive one another as quickly and thoroughly as God in Christ forgave you. (Ephesians 4:17–32, *The Message*)

10

When Change Is Needed but Not Wanted

FACING REALITIES WITH SOLUTIONS

"HOPE IS FRAGILE AND NEEDS TO BE TENDED AND RENEWED."
—Patrick Shade, *Habits of Hope*

Following my treatments and surgery, it became increasingly clear that some radical lifestyle changes were essential if recovery was to be complete. Dieticians talked with me about my diet, and doctors and pharmacists talked with me about medications and how important and risky they could be if mismanaged. Then physical therapists discussed an exercise routine... Well, you get the picture. Changes were needed and required if I were to experience health again. I confess, I did not want to do all they were recommending. I had to reflect on "counting the cost before building the tower." What would the consequences be if I didn't do what was recommended? My conclusion was not good, so I proceeded to live into the prescribed changes and routines to take me back to health.

A coaching client recently called me with some popular and focused issues:

- What is a good response when change is clearly needed but not wanted by the congregation or group?

- How do we respond when change is wanted but then not accepted by the core? What clues might help us respond well to each scenario?

The pastor had framed the congregation's issues well. We had an encouraging and enlightening coaching call. I asked if I could share some of our insights and gather some feedback from others.

Facing Realities in Churches
Today and Tomorrow

What a rapidly changing world we are in! I have spent the last twenty-eight years of my ministry exploring the impact of such a world on the way we do or do not do church. As soon as I think I have a handle on this subject, more changes emerge for the church to address. As a succinct summary of four of my books in one paragraph, here are some new realities facing many churches today and tomorrow.

- Growing diversity in our population base: the reality of a non-European immigrant population explosion in this country challenges every facet of church and community life in many places—suburban, urban, and rural.
- Growing secularization of the culture
- Growing disinterest in institutional and denominationally aligned churches
- Growing house-church worship
- Growing generational gaps and distinctive, personal preferences among a wide range of age groups
- Growing diversity of family relationships—from nonbiological to married with children, single parent, with or without children, same-sex, multicultural and multiethnic family systems, adopted and multicultural families, divorced, remarried, cohabitating, etc.
- Increasing scope and challenges of a 24–7 world
- Increased interest in spirituality from Eastern and Western perspectives
- Reframing of economic realities for families, communities, and churches
- ...And the list could go on

The point here is that almost every person, family, and congregation is facing at least one, if not more, of these changes. How individuals and groups choose to respond to the massive changes is as diverse as the changes themselves.

Prevalent Responses to Change

Response to change is often emotionally charged and runs all along a continuum of change.

- *Denial*–Some just stick their heads in the sand and deny that any changes are needed.
- *Rationalization*–Others rationalize, "If we don't change, we will die or become irrelevant and out of date."
- *Avoidance*–Some just dance around change, pretending that if they avoid the reality it will disappear.
- *Resistance*–Many, if not most, initially resist change. The old saying is, "No one likes change except a baby with a dirty diaper!" Some resist by fighting it. Others resist by withholding money or support. Still others resist by blaming the leaders and/or the pastor, while others resist by spiritualizing the situation and declaring, "God never changes and neither should we."
- *Embrace*–Some embrace change, even though they are uncomfortable with it, because they believe change is essential if the church and the mission of God are to be taken to their children and grandchildren in another generation. Others embrace change because they are strong people of faith and trust in God's Spirit to move the church forward. Others embrace because they are not fully satisfied with what is currently going on.

The purpose of this brief summary of changes and responses to change is to consider the clues a pastor or congregation might look for to help them assess where their leadership base and congregation are when it comes to understanding the need for change; the process of change; and the consequences, benefits, and challenges of change or of staying the same.

Pursuing Solutions to Resistance to Change in the Church

Change is a challenge for most organizations, particularly for churches. Businesses can mandate or impose change on their employees and expect employees to carry out the new changes. Churches, on the other hand, are primarily volunteer organizations that have deep history, tradition, and personal or family connections to the "way we do church here." So, pursuing solutions to resistance to change in church is an ongoing and essential skill set for most churches in this rapidly changing world. Conversations about change need to be consistent. Sermons and Bible studies about transformation, the mission of the church, and how the church impacts the world are needed often. Such conversations should be frequently explored and programmed. What is missing is consistent and ongoing dialogue about:

- What did congregation members hear?
- Where are the pinches (areas of discomfort) for you regarding change in the church?
- On a scale of 1 (completely closed) to 5 (totally open), where are you now in regards to openness to change?
- What is the Spirit saying to you? us?
- What shifts are needed in you? us?
- How can we make this change happen?

The power of congregational coaching is that it provides a safe and sacred process with an objective, nonjudgmental coach, committed to moving the church forward in light of the church's discernment of God's leadership. The process of congregational coaching, combined with a skilled, prayerful, and discerning coach can unlock pain, struggle, confusion, and power struggles, allowing recovery to begin and health and hope to be restored.

Resources to Consider for Possible Group Study

Hammett, Edward. *The Gathered and the Scattered Church.* Macon, Ga.: Smyth & Helwys, 1999.

_____. *Spiritual Leadership in a Secular Age.* Saint Louis: Chalice Press, 2005.

Hammett, Edward, and James Pierce. *Making Shifts without Making Waves.* Saint Louis: Chalice Press, 2009.

Suggested Resources for Next Steps

Go to www.transformingsolutions.org for other options and free downloadable podcasts around topics related to this chapter.

Invite an outside coach or consultant to visit your church with fresh eyes and to give feedback about how your church deals with outsiders.

Plan a sermon series and multigenerational dialogue/feedback groups in your church and community.

What else would help now?

Assessing the Viability of Change in a Church

CLUES CHANGE IS NEEDED	CLUES CHANGE IS NOT WANTED	POSSIBLE RESPONSES
Plateau or decline in attendance/participation	Comfort treasured Polarization of members; Us/them mentality "I pay the bills here" Value "come" structures	Visit other churches Create opportunity for casual dialogue
Growing irrelevancy for the context/population base	"Church is for members" mindset Personal preferences more valued than biblical mandates to go Insulation from community Tradition valued over mission	Plan windshield survey in community with key leaders Dialogue between groups and generations about personal preferences in music, spiritual formation, etc. Prayer walks in the community Getting clear about mission and tradition and the differences
Leader fatigue; church overprogrammed for active membership base	Tradition over appropriate or need Return to good old days "This is the way we have always done it" Just "be more committed," and it will work Problem is our pastor/ staff, not members Resistance to leaders or outside voice— "We can handle it"	Do an assessment: Is your church overprogrammed? Dialogue about value added and clear function of each activity/program of the church How does each program fuel the mission of the church? the biblical mandate for church? Assess how many leaders are leading out of "oughtness" vs. giftedness and calling Get clear about how each generation defines *commitment* How are we really doing now? evaluation/ dialogue

Minimal conversions or life transformation connected to church activities/focus	"Preacher's not doing the job" "Just need to be more committed" (but cannot tell you what that looks like) Programming valued more than end result of programming Resistance to rethinking "measuring what matters now"	Clarity about expectations of pastor/staff and members Clarity about what it means to be "more committed" Get clear about measuring what matters—metrics for your ministry and mission What are we trying "to do to people"? How do we know spiritual transformation is happening?
Inward focus of resources/staff, programming, and pastoral care	"Church is for me/us" values/mind-set Declaration of "friendly church'" but not practiced to outsiders Resistance to persons "not like us" Demanding attention by members, dislike sharing with outsiders Satisfied with *give* rather than *go* missions	Survey and walk to discover God in our community/culture How much of our resources/ budget, programming are primarily for "us"? for "them"? Dialogue about dealing with growing diversity in community, families, membership

11

The Power of Congregational Coaching

DISCOVERING/EMBRACING GOD'S FUTURE FOR YOUR CHURCH

"HOPE IS A STATE OF MIND, NOT OF THE WORLD.
HOPE, IN THIS DEEP AND POWERFUL SENSE, IS NOT THE SAME
AS JOY THAT THINGS ARE GOING WELL, OR WILLINGNESS TO INVEST
IN ENTERPRISES THAT ARE OBVIOUSLY HEADING FOR SUCCESS,
BUT RATHER AN ABILITY TO WORK FOR SOMETHING
BECAUSE IT IS GOOD."
—Vaclav Havel, *Disturbing the Peace*

You, the patient, have faced the realities of energy drain, deep fatigue, and a growing level of distraction. You have received health diagnosis and prognosis from specialists. Now the methodical treatment and challenging recovery begins. While this is true for the physical body, the same applies to the church desiring to be the faithful and fruitful body of Christ.

Congregational coaching is a pathway for congregations to face realities, discover resources they did not know they had, and discern God's leading in their midst. A coach can share the following introductory frameworks with those seeking to move forward and to discern the best strategy and leadership needed for them at this time. Some churches need consultants that are more direct and prescriptive; other churches need coaches who lead discernment and discovery processes that deepen ownership of new dreams and seek to move the church to action and mobilization.

Discovering and Embracing
God's Future for Your Church[1]
A COACH APPROACH TO STRATEGIC MINISTRY
FOR CHURCHES AND LEADERS

How would a coach approach look for your church? Certainly that is a major question ringing through your mind. Let's look at a coach's preliminary agenda and let you begin to see how a coach would want to work with you, and what might occur as a dedicated coach began to observe your church and perceive how relationships, programs, and in and outward concentrations and priorities actually take place among you, your community, and fellow members.

We will begin with a template process for Anywhere Church

ANYWHERE CHURCH—CONTRACT DATES

1. Process Overview for Building Ownership of New Dreams and Directions
2. Process Overview for Discovering Next Steps

A coach approach empowers churches and leaders to deal with current realities and prepare them for a positive missional and incarnational future. The coach works with the congregation and leaders to customize a process and strategy that works and brings hope for them Here's a possible map:

- Orientation–½ day with staff; ½ day with key leaders
- Coaching call with staff and key leaders
- Group discovery and declaration–all members: "What Is Our Current Reality?"

Discernment, assessment, and discovery of how/when/where culture may impact the way you do church in the next three-to-five years–five-hour workshop for key leaders and discovery team

- Interviews with community/church leaders/members–coaching call with interviewers
- Prayer triplets for church members (groups of three praying together for church and community) *(See guide for prayer on page 128.)*
- Interpreting data and discovery and commitment to next steps–five-hour workshop for staff, key leaders
- Coaching call for discovery team and staff
- Weekend celebration and sharing

Orientation

Target Group(s): Pastor and ministerial staff, key decision makers/leaders

DESIRED OUTCOMES

1. Discover and embrace our current reality–congregation, community, focus, priorities, intentionality, etc.
2. Identify people of influence in your community and congregation.
3. Clarify the current reality for the church from the community's and congregation's perspective.
4. What are the missional markers we need to embrace and focus on now?
5. Explore possible options for next steps with influencers and church and community leaders from desired outcome 2.
6. What are questions we need to explore with them?
7. Who can help us interview needed persons? by when?
8. Set direction about next steps needed in discernment.
9. Co-create strategy that will inform structure/organization for the future.
10. Begin praying for prayer triplet leaders and participants; clarify focus for prayers.

BENEFITS OF COACH APPROACH FOR THE CONGREGATION

- Builds ownership and leadership for future plans.
- Offers structure that is customized, collaborative, and relational.
- Forward focused rather than untangling past issues.
- Calls forth trust, spiritual discernment, collaboration, and clarity of focus.
- Shapes next steps, assignments that design a future story of impact and influence on the church and community.

COACH APPROACH STRATEGY
(Co-created by Target Leadership Groups)

1. What is working?
2. What is not working?
3. What are the options for next steps?
4. What do we need to know to move forward in the next three years?
5. Whom can we learn from?
6. Who needs to be involved in this strategy process?

7. Are there people who should not be involved? Why?
8. What else?

Half-day onsite coaching session with staff (four hours max; thirty-minute interview with secretary and ministerial staff)

Half-day onsite coaching session with key leaders (four hours max; staff not expected to participate) Key leaders are decision makers in your church leadership pool and those who are influencers and legitimizers.

Telephone Coaching Calls
(conference call about three weeks after the first meeting)

Target Group: Key leadership/pastor/staff –but open to any church member
Time Frame: One-hour call (more than one can be negotiated if needed)
Review of Coaching Covenant: Distinctives of the coach approach
Desired Outcomes, Tentative Focus

1. Check on progress
2. What would be most helpful for you now?
3. What are your wins?
4. What are your challenges?
5. What are next steps?
6. Prayer requests
7. What else?

Conference call number will be sent via e-mail to each target person. (Make sure the callers know they will be charged for the long-distance call by their local providers.)

DECISIONS ABOUT NEXT STEPS

1. _____
2. _____
3. _____

Culture Impact by 2020
(discuss about three-four weeks after first coaching call)

Target Group(s): Lead discovery team–pastor/staff, key leaders, any church member
(A discovery lead team are usually people of passion for the future of the church rather than just people of position. This team implements, along with the help of those in the congregation, the strategies discerned from the coaching process.)

Time: Three-to-four-hour workshop
Desired Outcomes
- Create a meaningful interview strategy–to be conducted by selected team.
- Frame interview questions by consensus.
- Co-create strategy that will inform structures/organizations for the future.
- Interviews will be conducted over a three-week period.
- Final summary of five-to-seven questions/responses will be sent to coach one week prior to interpretation meeting.
- Enlist team to facilitate prayer triplets among persons who do not know each other well. Have these triplet groups commit to praying for those interviewing and what they are hearing. Ask for six-week commitment to pray together by phone, over lunch, at a designated time at least once a week.
- Possible targets for interviews include: (Who? When? Where? How?)
    Music persons
    Staff
    Business owners
    Managers
    Blue-collar workers
    Students
    Faculty/administration of educational institutions
    Members of the medical community
    Government leaders
    Religious leaders
    Church leaders/members including all age groups

KEY COACHING QUESTIONS
1. What are you hearing that we need to remember?
2. What will likely be the challenges of the next three-to-five years?
3. What will likely be the opportunities of the next three-to-five years?
4. What is God saying to us now?
5. What do we need to do now to be prepared?
6. What else?

RESOURCE TO CONSIDER
Hammett, Edward. *Making the Church Work: Converting the Church for the 21st Century.* Macon, Ga.: Smyth & Helwys, 2000.

Interpreting Data
DISCERNMENT, DISCOVERY, AND COMMITMENT TO NEXT STEPS
(no longer than one month after interviews are finalized)

ASSESSMENT

- Summarize discoveries.
- Strategy informs structure.
- Clarify or change values before changing structure.
- Finalize plans/next steps needed.
- What is God saying to us now?
- Confirm commitments and make assignments.

ADJUSTMENTS CALLED FOR NOW

- What adjustments are needed in light of these discoveries?
    Forms
    Functions
    Structures
    Facilities
    Staffing
    Programs
    Administration Procedures and Policies
- What else?

Creating Our Future Story

FRAMEWORK FOR CELEBRATION SERVICE

What vision/strategy have we discovered? How can it be defined in no more than seven words?

What will our future story look like/sound like?

What shifts does this call for?
Staffing?
Organization?
Structures/Policies?
Direction?
Leadership Design?
What are our next steps into the future?
What else?

How can we share this future story in our celebration service?

How much will these changes cost?

Resources to Consider

Barry, William A. *Paying Attention to God: Discernment in Prayer.* Notre Dame, Ind.: Ave Marie Press, 1999.

_____. *Spiritual Direction and the Encounter with God.* Mahwah, N.J.: Paulist Press, 1992.

Bass, Dorothy C., ed. *Practicing Our Faith: A Way of Life for Searching People.* San Francisco: Jossey-Bass Publishers, 1997.

Bullard, George. *Pursuing the Full Kingdom Potential of Your Congregation.* Saint Louis: Chalice Press, 2008.

Farnham, Suzanne G., Joseph P. Gill, R. Taylor McLean, and Susan M. Ward. *Listening Hearts: Discerning Call in Community.* Harrisburg, Pa.: Morehouse Publishing, 1991.

Farnham, Suzanne G., Stephanie A. Hull, and R. Taylor McLean. *Grounded in God, rev. ed.: Listening Hearts: Discernment for Group Deliberations.* Harrisburg, Pa.: Morehouse Publishing, 1999.

Groff, Kent Ira. *The Soul of Tomorrow's Church: Weaving Spiritual Practices in Ministry Together.* Nashville: Upper Room Books. 2000.

Goleman, Daniel. Focus: *The Hidden Driver of Excellence.* New York: Harper Collins. 2013.

Hammett, Edward. *Spiritual Leadership in a Secular World.* Saint Louis: Chalice Press, 2007.

Hammett, Edward, and James Pierce. *Making Shifts without Making Waves.* St. Louis: Chalice Press, 2009.

Hamm, Dick. *Recreating Your Church.* Saint Louis: Chalice Press, 2008.

Hamrick, Terry. *Leadership in Constant Change: Embracing a New Missional Reality.* Atlanta: Cooperative Baptist Fellowship, 2012.

LaBarre, Glynis. *Learning Mission, Living Mission: Churches that Work.* Valley Forge, Pa.: Judson Press. 2012.

Melander, Rochelle, and Harold Eppley. *Growing Together: Spiritual Exercises for Church Committees.* Minneapolis, Minn.: Augsburg Fortress Press, 1998.

Morris, Danny E., and Charles M. Olsen. *Discerning God's Will Together: A Spiritual Practice for the Church.* Nashville: The Alban Institute with Upper Room Books, 1997.

Ogden, Greg. *Leadership Essentials: Shaping Vision, Building Character, Multiplying Influence.* Downers Grove, Ill.: InterVarsity Press, 2007.

Olsen, Charles M. *Transforming Church Boards into Communities of Spiritual Leaders.* Bethesda, Md.: The Alban Institute, 1995.

Rogers, Roberta. *Is That You, Lord?: Practical Methods for Learning Spiritual Discernment.* Grand Rapids, Mich.: Chosen Books, 2000.

Smith, Gordon T. *Listening to God in Times of Choice: The Art of Discerning God's Will.* Downers Grove, Ill.: InterVarsity Press, 1997.

Stevens, Garrie, Pamela Lardear, and Sharon Duger. *Seeking and Doing God's Will: Discernment for the Community of Faith.* Nashville: Discipleship Resources, 1998.

Woods, Jeff. *On the Move: Adding Strength, Balance, and Speed to Your Congregation.* Saint Louis: Chalice Press, 2010.

12

New Dance Steps in Ministry

LEARNING TO ENJOY NEW CHALLENGES

"WHERE THERE IS NO HOPE THERE CAN BE NO ENDEAVOR."
—Eliza Cook, *Diamond Dust*

Living into new health realities calls us to new behaviors, new skills, and new standards for making decisions that move us to better physical or organizational health. When health challenges appear, are acknowledged, diagnosed, and treated, the hard work of recovery and life change begins. The patient must live into the new realities of a new health. Unless the patient implements these changes, life is not likely to improve, and pathological symptoms recur. The newness is often like a dance moving from a slow waltz to modern rock, seeking to balance what has been comfortable in the past and what is best for us now. The dance is often not easy, especially for people like me, who like familiarity and routine. Now the familiarity and routine are going to have to change to new familiarities and new routines. The new dance steps were "challenging," at best, but I realized they were essential if recovery were to become a reality.

Churches may not be the best dance instructors. Members are often too self-conscious or inward focused to join the dance. Coachable congregations are ready to take a chance, even if they fall or someone laughs at them. They may even join the laughter and embrace the challenge. On the other hand, ministers and churches may resonate with the following confessions:

- "I'm not having much fun anymore in my ministry."
- "I'm just not making the impact I want to make in ministry."
- "I feel like I'm dancing with two left feet stumbling all over myself and others."
- My dance skills are just not what they use to be. I need some new dance steps for my ministry."
- "The flow of ministry is gone. It has become more work with less fulfillment and fun."
- "If I don't find relief, I'm going to have to find another career."

These are actual statements I have heard more than once from persons and churches I am privileged to coach. The first time I heard the metaphor of dance connected with ministry it was somewhat of a disconnect for me; but, the more I thought about it, the more sense it made. Ministry is filled with disconnects these days, and multiple challenges take many of us beyond our comfort zones, as is true for many dancers.

Discovering and Dealing with Disconnects in Ministry

WHAT ARE THE MINISTRY DISCONNECTS TODAY?

A ministry disconnect is countercultural from what has worked to build traditional churches in a church-oriented culture (prior to the 1960s) and what seems to be essential in today's post-Christian culture. I often encounter these disconnects:

Caregiving does not build churches. For those born prior to 1960, the essence of an effective church was one that cared for its members. Weddings, funerals, hospital and home visitation, and programming were designed for members. If a leader and congregation did this well, the church grew. Today that does not work as consistently. In fact, outsiders often perceive the church's care as merely self-serving, self-focused, maintenance oriented, and against missional interests of many of those seeking church today.

Preaching no longer attracts members. Those born before 1960 placed a high value on biblical and relevant preaching. A great preacher could grow a church and attract members. That is no longer the only ingredient for an effective church that attracts members (particularly those born after the 1960s). What attracts people today has as much if not more to do with the power of community-building experiences than preaching experiences. The sermon is not the message; service is the message.

Christian education is not a program; it is an experience with believers. Christian education, and the five dimensions of programming around the five functions of a church (worship, discipleship, evangelism, education, outreach), is fading in many places. In other places, time-starved people are demanding streamlining and simplifying of church. The five functions are giving way to one or two structures designed to create, interpret, and mobilize experiences with Christians in spontaneous and planned encounters.

Worship hinges on God-focused activity, not necessarily church-focused activities. Many today crave worship. From the church and its worship, persons seek meaning and motivation preparing them to live through rapid change, increasing diversity, and a world that often moves so fast that connection with the Divine is a challenge at best. Worship today is God-focused activity found in the normal course of one's busy life, pausing periodically and intentionally to reflect and recenter a life. Such is often found in corporate worship in a gathered community, but not often in church-focused programming or activities many of us valued in days gone by.

A full program for all ages and niches may be more a hindrance for spiritual formation than a facilitator for it. With fractured and busy families, an age-graded, multi-tiered program to facilitate spiritual formation is often a hindrance or distraction rather than a facilitator of spiritual growth. Today many are seeking safe places to struggle with tough issues that happen in the busyness and spontaneity of daily life. Creating safe relationships becomes the need and service that is valued. Maybe we are in a day when we have coaches on call and life coaches available throughout workplaces, cities, schools, and communities. The scattered church may be surfacing in God's design once again.

Building church is more about building partnerships and relationships than membership, staff, and buildings. In days gone by, the institutional church was built through building buildings to house growing memberships. Today churches are created through relationship building and facilitating partnerships that are redemptive, restorative, and missional focused. The church today will be more mission driven than membership driven.

New Dance Steps for More Effective Ministry

Some in the pulpit and pew would question putting dancing and ministry in the same sentence; however, allow me to continue to use the metaphor to help us discover new steps that can return the joy to ministry in spite of the challenges we face today.

As I listen to many pastors struggle with their effectiveness and sense of competence, some patterns emerge. These patterns are restoring the joy and effectiveness of ministry for many clergy and churches across the country. Permit me to share some of the new dance steps my coaching clients are discovering and teaching me.

What new dance steps are needed for more enjoyable and fruitful ministry today?

Flexibility is a must today. Increasing diversity, faster pace of change, and changing patterns of family—among other things—bring great challenge to many. The traditional and basic waltz steps (skills, routines) of ministry are no longer sufficient. Being flexible in routine, learning to create multiple entry points for worship, spiritual formation, and coaching offer new hope and options for many searching for something new.

Openness to new routines, schedules, new voices, rituals, styles, and communication venues restores the destabilized dancer. So often pastors and other staff and lay leaders are stuck in one or two basic routines for worship planning and for communicating with the congregation and leadership teams. "Let's call a meeting at the church" is now being replaced by, "Let's meet over Skype or on a conference call." Printed orders of service and announcements are being replaced or at least supplemented through Facebook pages for the church, websites, and online learning opportunities. Being open and willing to face and embrace these steep learning curves creates energy, connects with another generation, and often expedites and broadens leadership.

Pruning is one of the most challenging new dance steps. Pruning is essential for fruit bearing. Many churches and leaders are not bearing fruit in their ministry because they fear pruning ineffective volunteer leaders who are not on the same page with church leadership and with a changing church mission. Churches and ministers must have the courage to disenfranchise people who prove themselves to be consistent distracters and unreliable participants/leaders of the church's programs and activities. Pruning could also relate to pruning the bad habits of the pastor/staff or lay leaders. Change is not easy, but often essential to bear fruit. Pruning might also relate to downsizing activities and programming, and to decentralizing planning to make ministry more convenient for attendees.

Creating partnerships is another essential new dance move. Seeking out and creating new partnerships for ministry brings excitement, additional resourcing of people and funds, and broadens the leadership base. This is a real new move for many and is often questioned. Those who learn this new step benefit greatly in leadership, ownership of new dreams, and resourcing.

Building relationships maximizes bridge building and minimizes creating barriers with those inside and outside the church walls. So much focus in some churches is on setting the church apart and against people, lifestyles, or practices rather than learning to be in the world but not of the world. When barriers are created and persons are turned away, the church severs any possibility of reaching those people. Learn to practice Christian congeniality and confidence, not division and denial.

"Forward focus"–faithing it, not faking it–is the needed new motto. Let's face it–some churches and leaders believe in the motto, "Fake it 'til you make it." That does not work and certainly does not move things forward. So often the new step is relying on faith more and staying forward focused rather than watching our footsteps from the past. A smooth, confident dancer flows with faith in relationships, skills, and choreography. Surely pastors and key leaders should do no less.

Remnant focus is another needed new step for leaders and one that goes against the tradition and against most leaders' comfort zones. Jesus preached to the multitude but invested himself in the remnant, those few who were willing to follow. What would really happen if we as churches and pastors/staff followed the disciple-making model found consistently in Jesus' ministry?

Creativity is needed as never before. Things are changing exponentially in the world. Certainly I am not advocating changing the gospel message. I am encouraging trusting the Spirit, being willing to follow into creative avenues that open before us. Creativity is a challenge for many of us; it stretches us into learning to use technology, stories, media clips, new ways of measuring effectiveness and success, and new ways of framing partnerships and conducting meetings, worship, and celebrating holy days.

Discernment is a spiritual gift that is so powerful and so needed in this new generation. Discernment is learning to recognize, discover, and embrace the movement of the Holy Spirit, looking for connections and disconnections as teachable moments or divine appointments. Learning to connect with and trust the leadership of one's curiosity and intuition, recognizing them as fueled by the Spirit, is empowering to all those we dance among.

Hope-building, restoration ministries rather than judgment are needed today. Those who are broken, wounded, skeptical, or riddled with dysfunction or addictions need hope. Learning to create, nurture, and sustain restoration relationships, structures, and environments is crucial. This really is the music that creates the proper atmosphere for great dance moves. Without the right atmosphere great dancing is empty.

Coaching your church rather than carrying your church offers great relief to clergy and empowerment and opportunity for lay leaders! The coach approach is not about being seen as the expert, fixer, or answer person. Coaching is about helping others discern, discover, and move forward into actions that align with belief systems. The coach approach creates sacred space and place for persons to slow down, listen, and connect the dots of what God is bringing forth in their lives. It really does work! This offers another tool in the toolkit. It's a tool I wish I had known about thirty years ago when my ministry began!

Restore the joy, face challenges with faith not fear, and enjoy the music and relief of working with partners who embrace the same dance and look forward to the same hope. *(For additional resources, downloadable podcasts, webinars, and e-zines on many of these issues, visit my websites.)*

When a church realizes today's church is not the same as it was for their parents and grandparents, and when that church and its leaders are open and ready to embrace the future, that church may be a prime candidate to benefit from a coach approach.

One indication of a church that might benefit from coaching is when a congregation realizes it is not growing in numbers or in spiritual maturity, when the people realize that new people rarely come and, even more infrequently, join and stay. The church has begun to wonder if all the fault lies with the outsiders or if those inside the church may not be as welcoming as they had supposed. A coach can lead them to consider whether the congregation has become a clique, and what they can do to change that image.

New dance steps call forth new assessment and measuring tools and a fresh understanding of a twenty-first–century culture. Such new steps will help reveal what creating a new church culture will look like. Following the treatment and recovery, the church is ready to plan to move toward deeper health and greater effectiveness. Such movement often calls for a shift in culture for leaders and for the church body. Now the question becomes, What type of culture is needed to move us forward?

13

When Leaders Change, Churches Change

"THE GREATEST ARCHITECT AND THE ONE MOST NEEDED IS HOPE."
—Henry Ward Beecher, *Proverbs from Plymouth Pulpit*

I come from a family of church leaders. I have served in volunteer, part-time, full-time, and multi-career leadership positions in churches, denominations, and parachurch groups. I have seen and experienced the challenges and the celebrations of leadership. Throughout the last forty-plus years of service, I have noted and felt the pressures to care for the flock.

Too often culture expectations of members—and even of the church leadership—focus on caring for the members through deep and wide pastoral care. Hospital, nursing home, and home visitation are essential in most churches—particularly those under 350 in attendance. Then, of course, marriages, counseling sessions, crisis counseling, funerals, and follow-up bereavement care and counseling fill church calendars. We might also mention membership and spiritual formation counseling. If the pastoral leaders, deacons, and elders do all the expected caring, we have little time to lead the church forward. There's only so much time in a day and so much energy.

After decades of consulting with churches of all sizes and denominational affiliations, I am convinced that *many churches stay stuck in a plateaued attendance pattern because they choose not to change their expectations for church and pastoral leaders.* When clergy are expected to do most of the caregiving, the church decides to become plateaued and stuck in a maintenance posture, leaving little hope for engaging the unchurched around them. Members expect pastoral care from the clergy. In fact, some often remind the pastor, "We deserve to be cared for. After all, we do pay the bills around here!"

For a church to grow, church leaders have to do more than care for the flock. They must lead forward. *Church leaders and congregations need to understand that pastoral care can be provided in a variety of ways to minimize the caregiving expectations on the pastor/staff and deacon leadership in order that key leaders might focus on leading the church forward into the future. Unless the church expectations shift, the pastoral care model cannot shift.* Leadership is about moving forward, not just pampering the pews or pacifying the saints and sinners of the church. How can you provide adequate pastoral care while you provide leadership into a bright future for the church?

Church Leadership Needed in Twenty-First–Century Churches

I want to summarize ten characteristics needed by effective key leaders if churches are to move forward in mission in our current culture. *(For more information, go to www.TransformingSolutions.org for other published resources on the topics here.)*

1. *Leaders mobilize laypersons in ministry.* Many lay leaders are or can be great at pastoral care. Ephesians 4:12 declares, "Equip the saints for the work of ministry" (NRSV). Lay members are gifted with mercy, helping, nurturing, and teaching, and can do a great job if the congregational culture values their calling and validates their caregiving.

2. *Leaders build partnerships and alliances* in the surrounding community. (An example of this would be how First Baptist Church of Wilmington, North Carolina, created partnerships and alliances with social service agencies and other churches to care for the needs of their inner city. Recently they hosted a prayer breakfast for those in city government who wanted to participate.) This gives people opportunities to be salt, light, and leaven in the world and to be leaders of impact and influence in community groups or businesses.

3. *Leaders spend time with other leaders* to build relationships, stay current, and engage persons by forming short-term task-force teams. Effective teams complete projects for the good of the community.

4. *Leaders model Christlike behavior among believers and nonbelievers.* Leaders need to spend time with other leaders and with nonbelievers as models for laity to do the same.

5. *Leaders who are pastors/ministers are called to lead* in worship on a regular basis, but such leadership roles can also be shared with lay ministers if the church culture values this and validates their leadership roles.

6. *Leaders have to be engaged in intentional prayer, reflection, and continuing education* to stay focused and connected with rapid shifts in culture and new discoveries that impact the spiritual health of church leaders and members.

7. *Leaders are disciple makers* who grow people in faith and fruitfulness. Where faith matures, leaders are being fruitful and multiplying ministry.

8. *Leaders lead.* If leaders only provide care, then the church is likely to become more inward focused than outward focused on accomplishing the biblical mandate for the church.

9. *Leaders are responsible for moving the church forward,* pleasing God and not just caring for the needs of members.

10. *Leaders are called to stretch beyond their comfort zones* to model growth, maturity, and faith as God pulls the church and leaders toward higher heights and deeper depths of the love of God.

Change in Leadership Changes Churches

Making a change in leadership changes a church or any organization. Leaders get stale, comfortable, content, and secure. This often provides the seeds of an inward-focused, content- and maintenance-focused congregation. Leadership change can mean a change of persons with different skill sets and vision, or it can be a change in leadership focus, priorities, and philosophy for the leadership core. As organizations grow in number, diversity, and challenge, they need a different leadership focus and sometimes a different leadership direction. Discerning when, how, and at what pace such leadership shifts need to be made often requires an outsider's perspective—a congregational coach or consultant who brings fresh eyes and ears to the situation.

On more than a few occasions, I have seen churches avoid these tough, yet obvious, leadership shift issues just to preserve harmony in the church. I am not against harmony at all, but the mission of the church in the twenty-first century cannot afford to be stuck in maintenance mode if it wants to fulfill the Great Commission.

Let me close with a few leadership shifts needed in some pastors and/or core leaders in maintenance-oriented churches. Such churches need leaders

- who lead into the future with courage, hope, and faith rather than with fear and appeasement;
- who organize to provide pastoral care for members through gifted lay ministers while key leaders are primarily engaged in moving the church forward;
- who cultivate community relationships and partnerships that ensure an incarnational and missional presence of Christ outside the church;
- who create meeting agendas that maximize improving the church's Christlike impact and influence in the world rather than agendas that keep the machine of the church running;
- who work from passion, calling, and gifting rather than leaders recruited on the basis of "oughtness" brought on by a tradition that requires a committtee to fill vacant positions in the church;
- who acknowledge and plan for a realistic and appropriate balance of time, energy, and resources on church work (day-to-day operations of church) *and* the work of the church (the Great Commission).

More often than not, when a church rests on a plateau for several years, it is receiving a clear signal that the leadership style of the church, and maybe its structure and policies, need to shift. Rather than embracing the signal to reassess leadership style and policies, many church members begin to blame the pastor, staff, community demographics, apathy of the membership, or even lack of commitment. While there may be some truth leading to such blame, more often than not I see the blame as a rationalization that distracts the church from rethinking and reframing ministry and leadership style.

COACHING QUESTIONS
1. What is the Spirit saying to you now? How does this chapter speak to you or your church?
2. What characteristics of the leadership of your church may indicate the need for a shift in leadership style?
3. Does blame or claim to mission characterize your church?
4. Which of the ten leadership characteristics mark the staff and lay leadership of your church?
5. In what way is tradition preventing your church from Focusing Forward?

14

Culture—Not Numbers—Matters Now

WHAT KEEPS MAINLINE CHURCHES STUCK?

"WHAT WE CALL OUR DESPAIR IS OFTEN
ONLY THE PAINFUL EAGERNESS OF UNFED HOPE."
—George Eliot, *Middlemarch*

Once a heart patient, always a heart patient is a reality I have grown to accept. If I am to stay healthy, I have to adopt certain attitudes, behaviors, tests, diets, and routines to ensure ongoing health. Such a realization proved a major shift of heart and mind for me. The realization also demanded a shift in my priorities for my time, energy, and money. Health suddenly became the priority by which all other decisions are made.

Similarly, church health is a major issue. Many are asking, "What makes a mainline moderate church grow or not grow?" Pastors, denominational and judicatory executives, church staff, and church members across the country are asking this question. Some are increasingly curious as to why most mainline denominations are decreasing in membership while Churches of God, Pentecostals, Latter-Day Saints, and Jehovah's Witnesses are showing increases in membership numbers. What causes some congregations to grow and others to decline or get stuck?

Some answer this question by saying it is about demographic shifts. Others suggest it is a leadership issue. Still others say it is about an increasingly secular culture. And others say some churches are "cooking the books" when it comes to counting numbers attending or participating. While all of these are pieces of the explanation, I would like to suggest that the issue of growing and declining churches centers around *the culture of the congregation,* or the lack thereof. Church culture contributes significantly to attracting others to or discouraging people from church attendance or membership.

Many churches announce, "Come join the friendliest church in town," but guests experience anything but friendliness when they encounter the members on the streets during the week or in the pews on Sunday. When this happens, not only are some discouraged from membership, but they also experience a disconnect between what the church professes and what they practice. This causes an outsider to label the church as closed, cold, hypocritical, or lacking authenticity. Their experience with the congregation (inside or outside the church walls) overrides what the congregation professes in their statement of beliefs, core values, or doctrine.

Many moderate mainline congregations are so afraid of being perceived or experienced as dictatorial, rigid, or controlling in leadership style that leaders intellectualize and articulate with great precision beliefs without intentional attention to aligning voiced beliefs with congregational behaviors. Creating a church culture calls for intentional, focused, prayerful, and active leadership from the pulpit and the pew if beliefs and behaviors are to be aligned into a powerful community of faith. Consider some barriers and bridges to an inviting culture.

Elements in a Church's Culture That Diminish or Deter Interest of Possible New Members

- Initiative for inviting and welcoming comes primarily from clergy rather than from members.
- Invitation and welcoming opportunities are limited to church facilities and functions rather than designed in community experiences.
- Members' attitude of judgment about lifestyle, dress, relationships, and worship style practices is communicated, if not spoken.
- Spoken or unspoken dress code is in place for church events rather than truly welcoming and accepting people just as they are.
- Avoiding eye contact with one another and with nonmembers is common.

- Members resist or avoid encounters with persons they do not know.
- Members avoid learning new names, families, and interests of newcomers and members not in their comfort zone of relationships.
- Members are unintentional about widening their fellowship circle to include persons different from them.
- People expend more energy preserving their comfort zone of relationships and personal preferences than on building new interests with new persons/families.
- Members resist to creating new units/groups that are designed to be comfortable entry points for others.
- Blaming the pastor(s) for membership decline only fuels apathy and comfort in the pews.
- Membership policies and practices preserve passivity in the pews rather than intentionality in relationship building and spiritual maturity that impacts the community.
- The membership is more focused on institutional and self-comfort preservation than connecting Christ to the community and to mobilizing community as the church in the world.

Elements of a Growth-Oriented Church Culture That Attract/Invite Possible New Members

- Members' intentional, invitational, and welcoming acts and attitudes reach out and welcome outsiders and other members.
- Members and staff continually stay intentional about calling persons by name and about networking with others, sharing similar work, community, recreation, school, or leisure experiences.
- An attitude of nonjudgment marks the words and actions of the pastor and congregation toward differences of personal preferences in dress, worship styles, and music.
- Congregation exhibits openness and willingness to build new relationships with persons outside their comfort zone or pathways.
- Church practices willingness and intentionality in making room for newcomers in classrooms, groups, families, and relationships.
- People daily act with intentionality about being the presence of Christ and church in the community in which they work, play, and reside.

- Members consciously and intentionally exhibit the gifts and fruit of the Spirit in all relationships in work, worship, play, and community life.
- People create sacred space and relationships that nurture one's distinctive spiritual journey, faith formation, and missional engagement whenever possible.
- Church focuses on creating opportunities for churched and unchurched persons to connect, fellowship, and engage in projects of mutual interest.
- Church holds nurturing, hope-building, nonjudgmental attitudes among churched and unchurched relationships.
- Membership prayerfully and intentionally invites nonbelievers, churched, and unchurched persons to share their skills, expertise, and gifts in family, community, and church projects as often as possible.
- Congregation consistently and continuously prays and seeks to be attentive to the work and leadership of the Holy Spirit, seeing relationships as divine appointments and teachable moments created by the Spirit.
- Church looks for and designs opportunities to create spiritual anchors and coaching relationships in community and social gatherings.

Great facilities, age-graded programming, skilled pastoral leadership, and eloquence in the pulpit will no longer grow a church. The culture and pastoral care of the church, created and sustained by members and attendees, contributes more to achieving and sustaining numerical and spiritual growth than pastor, church staff, or well-designed facilities. Learning to be prayerful, intentional, and purposeful in creating a growth-oriented church culture calls for courageous and visionary leadership fueled by prayer, discernment, creativity, openness, and powerful faith.

Leaders and churches that want to be intentional about creating a growth-oriented culture will certainly challenge the status quo, comfort zones, and personal preferences of many of their existing members. Learning to create a new culture in a congregation calls for a refined skill set of introducing and managing change and transition. My book *Making Shifts without Making Waves: A Coach Approach to Soulful Leadership* provides practical tools and ideas for leaders and congregations who are ready to begin this transformational journey of faith and courage.

Denominations or churches experiencing growth are often more intentional about creating a church culture that nurtures community, family life, and impact on the community in which they are located. Some mainline churches are more interested in creating a culture that preserves comfort zones and insulates outsiders from insiders. These churches focus more on proclamation to members than creating places and space for proclaiming to newcomers and outsiders. In fact, some mainline congregations are more focused on pampering the pew (keeping the members happy) than penetrating the community with the good news.

A rural United Methodist Church in Tennessee is moving from maintenance to mission to incarnational ministry design. Their pastor, Ginger Howe, celebrates:

> The partnerships in our community are coming right along. We have had a very busy couple of months! I went to Chattanooga with the Master Gardeners to look at some community gardens, and we are hoping to work together in developing a community garden in the neighborhood that has been one of our targets for outreach. We had our last movie night with Rural Resources in April, and we are hoping to co-host a Community Table this summer downtown, inviting the community to one giant covered dish focusing on locally grown produce. This coming Saturday we are co-sponsoring a Wellness Fair in the parking lot of the local community college, capitalizing on foot traffic downtown during the annual Iris Festival. This came out of a Bible study we did last summer, and Rural Resources and another UMC have partnered with us on this endeavor. We have at least twenty health-related organizations and agencies that will be participating, which we feel is phenomenal since this is the first year we are doing this! We just finished up our Greene County History Week events, our church hosting two of the events, and the History Week committee was most pleased with what we offered. We were the only church in town invited to take part in this inaugural event, so we felt very honored with the invitation. The crafters day continues to be a welcomed venue for residents. So, with everything we have had going on, the church has been in the local paper quite a bit these past few weeks. I'm beginning to hear residents in the community talk about how involved we are in our community.
>
> We are still exploring the house church concept. The Cal-Pac Annual Conference has an elder appointed to a house church network, so I want to call her and talk with her in the next couple of weeks about her training process for leadership and how they organize the house churches. And, after VBS, we hope to use a local park in our target neighborhood for our Sunday evening worship during the summer.

We are slowly starting to build those relationships that I pray will lead to fruitful change for both the church and those whom we are embracing in our outreach.

I do hope you will be able to return to our district for a follow-up. I will be praying about that. Thank you so much for your prayers and interest in our ministry. That means a lot to me!

Two weeks after this first e-mail, the UMC pastor sent me another exciting update that indicates God is up to something in rural Tennessee. I share her excitement with her permission. She declares:

A new opportunity presented itself today. I received a phone call from a gentleman, Jeff, that used to run a computer repair business and who has worked on my computers in the past couple of years. Recently, he and a couple of other guys started an Internet radio station called This Is Greeneville. One of his partners, John, runs a sound business and does sound for local concerts and also installs sound systems (he installed ours at the church), and he and Greg, my husband, have recently become buds over trying to make some things happen downtown. The third guy is a former DJ at a traditional AM radio station that airs a tape of my Sunday morning sermons.

They have invited me to have an hour spot on the station once a week. It would be a call-in show, and they want to keep it positive. Jeff said they just felt like their listeners needed a show that offered spiritual encouragement, and they see me as being a positive voice in town.

Both Jeff and John have been part of the downtown meetings I have recently been attending. Interestingly, neither attend a church. I have a SPRC meeting Friday so we will talk about it there, but I hope the church will be supportive of it.

Just wanted to let you know the latest.

Such stories bring me great hope that God is doing a new work in large and small churches, in city and suburban and rural congregations, in congregations with men and with women as pastors. God is doing a new work with white, Asian, African-American, Hispanic, and any other ethic or cultural group. Congregations committed to God's mission and open to the movement of the Spirit represent the future of God's church. Churches caught in temple rather than tabernacle spirituality will likely decrease in number and impact. Those with an organic, open, flexible, and responsive people will thrive in impact and number in the future.

Until leaders and congregations of faith acknowledge errors, disconnects, and areas of resistance, many churches will continue to decline in impact, influence, and membership. I reflect on the writings of the apostle Paul, who was the chief agent of God in starting new churches in a very unchurched and highly secular culture. The book of Acts, along with Paul's writings, suggest he went to great lengths to make changes in dress, diet, traditions, and even personal preferences so that he (a Jew) could be used by God to reach those unlike him (Gentiles). Maybe we are being called to the same level of commitment, creativity, and courage. His churches were not in the synagogue as much as they were in storefronts, homes, and community gatherings. Albert Einstein explained, "Logic gets you from A to B; imagination gets you everywhere." Could it be that this has something to say about why the house church movement is growing across the world while many institutional churches are struggling in these difficult days of change and economic challenges?

A dear friend and pastor, Ronny Russell, who has been walking his church from maintenance to mission, put this chart together, giving brief descriptors of temple and tabernacle spirituality. Consider his work and evaluate how you see and experience church in your life and in your ministry context. What is the Spirit saying to you?

Temple or Tabernacle...or Both?

© 2006 by Ronny Russell

A TEMPLE SPIRITUALITY	A TABERNACLE SPIRITUALITY
Church is something you come to.	Church is something you do.
Limited number of participants in ministry.	Everyone can participate in ministry.
Bible study is an option.	Bible study is a necessity for everyone in ministry on the front lines.
Scripture is relevant only when the people are gathered.	Scripture is increasingly relevant for people gathered and scattered.
Says, "We can't go to the mission fields but we can send others."	Says, "Why can't we go?"
The temple was David's idea (2 Sam. 7:5–7).	The tabernacle was God's idea (Num. 9:18–23).
The temple culture is a safe and well-charted place.	The roads are less traveled and frequently are not on the map.
Revolves around buildings.	Revolves around the road.

Represents settled religion.	Represents mobile religion.
A spirituality for the familiar places and well-traveled paths.	A spirituality for the unfamiliar places and new vistas.
A spirituality for the people on the inside.	A spirituality for exiles and marginalized.
Longs for certainty and security.	Lives by innovation and experiment.
Employs priests to minister in the temple.	Deploys priests for the road.
The prophet is unheard and unwelcomed.	The message of the prophet is welcomed for its poignancy.
Reliance on priests.	Reliance on the Word.
Values comfort and security for the sake of the temple.	Sacrifices comfort and security for the sake of the kingdom.
God is pretty much limited to a sacred space.	Every place is potentially sacred space—we take God with us.
Buildings are fixed, and they tend to create us in their image.	Has great flexibility and ability to respond to change.
Has a mortgage and a priest to support.	Depends on what God is doing and where he is doing it.
An accommodation that God didn't want because He is static.	A picture of how God dwells with his people—God is on the move.
Built in cleared and domesticated places.	Built in the wilderness, a metaphor for wild places.
Must be attractive to bring in people from the outside.	Must be with people wherever they are.
Like a huge train, not easy to turn around.	Is already turned.

© Ronny Russell www.live-againministries.org

I am not asking for agreement with my or Ronny's thinking as much as dialogue about these explanations and challenges. I welcome any illustration, challenge, or insight as the concepts continue to clarify in my mind, heart, and practice.

COACHING QUESTIONS

1. After reviewing the elements outlined, how does your church rate in each category?
2. What would you add to each category?
3. What actions need to be taken to improve the culture of your congregation in the next decade?

4. What are you willing to do now to move this dialogue into action in your church?

Finding Focus Births Clear Metrics
(What Will It Take to Make This Happen?)

As congregational coaching unfolds, leaders commonly become highly aware and often concerned that a new system of measurement and evaluation needs to be put in place. The measurement system of days gone by is not as effective in assessing the impact, influence, and missional and incarnational momentum we need. Below is one congregation's metrics based on their congregational coaching process. Your metric may be similar or entirely different.

Metrics for Missional Congregations
(Creating and Sustaining Missional Momentum)

PRAYERFULLY AND INTENTIONALLY PLAN, CONDUCT, AND EVALUATE:

- Increased number of go structures (beyond the walls of the church)
- Balance of come (inside church programming and building) and go structures
- Number of nonbelievers, key leaders, pastor/staff engaging in meaningful relationships
- Number of nonchurched persons, key leaders, pastor/staff, and members of congregation engaging in meaningful relationships
- Number of unchurched persons who welcome you into their worlds
- Amount of time/energy/resources spent on discovering and engaging the unchurched as compared to that spent maintaining the church community
- Number of new (previously unknown) family systems with whom you engage in meaningful, consistent relationships
- Number of persons you personally invite to join you in a church-sponsored event
- Number of unchurched you invite and engage in mission experiences (eg., mission trips, Habitat House construction, community festival events)
- Number of leaders you commission as missionaries in their vocations, community activities (volunteers)
- Number of partnerships you discover and build that provide avenues of ministry opportunities

- Number of church families who invite their neighbors into their homes for fellowship (4 x 4 groups, cookouts, ice cream)
- The power of transformational stories shared in families, worship, and communities
- The images and indicators of reconciliation, redemption, and hope that are shared and embraced by church and community
- What else?

NEW METRICS WE AGREE TO FOLLOW AND ENTHUSIASTICALLY EMBRACE

Another common issue emerges and is often the toughest part of the congregational coaching journey. Leaders begin to see that new things are emerging that will move them forward, but people ask, How are we going to do more than we are doing now? *This process is not intended to layer more onto leaders, staff, pastor, or congregational members.* Finding focus, prioritizing, and establishing new methods of evaluation generate a need to stop doing some things so you can focus on what needs to be done now. This acrostic might be of help as you learn to say no to some things so you can say yes to the priorities established through congregational coaching. The journey of recovery calls for accountability and consistent monitoring by trained persons to build in new values and lifestyle habits to ensure improvement and health.

Focusing a Congregation's Strategy Exercise
Willingness to "Create in Me a New Heart, O God" (Ps. 51:10).

F ree Space, Resources, Time (What Do You Stop Doing to Focus on Priorities?)

_____
_____
_____

O penness to Focus, Consensus, Forward Movement (How to Move Together?)

_____
_____
_____

C larifying Direction (What Are Emerging as Priorities?)

_____

_____

_____

U ndergird with Focused Intentional Prayer (What Is the Spirit
Saying about Next Steps?)

_____

_____

_____

S elect Two Churchwide Priorities Each Year (or Every Six
Months) That Align with Church Mission/Vision (List Two Priorities You Recommend)

_____

_____

_____

Finding focus and priority creates hope and direction. We know
who we are, where we are going, and who and how we can get
there. That is a super hope builder for many inside and outside the
church walls. A congregation can work toward other hope builders
as momentum builds and leaders and congregation embrace God's
dream for the future of the church.

15

Creating Hope
Builders in Your Church

"GOD PUTS THE EXCESS OF HOPE IN ONE MAN,
IN ORDER THAT IT MAY BE A MEDICINE
TO THE MAN WHO IS DESPONDENT."
—Henry Ward Beecher, *Proverbs from Plymouth Pulpit*

In the midst of health recovery, one seeks hope—hope that things will get better, that energy will return, that engagement with life's pleasures will present themselves once again. Hope is critical, particularly on those days when discouragement comes with new life experiences that are not so comfortable but are prescribed. Hope is needed when you do not see things getting better fast enough. I recall feeling this a number of times as I was hooked up to heart monitors during the rehabilitation exercise time. What a hassle! How uncomfortable! But it did give me some security to push myself to strengthen my muscles after being bedridden for about six months. Churches in recovery also need to cling to hope that things will get better if they stay on course with treatment and new lifestyle choices.

No doubt the hope of the church is Christ. Where do churches go to connect with aspects of hope that move them forward? Hope is found in honesty, exploring possibilities, options, and how to identify and move through barriers. Hope is anchored in the promises of God, but also in the hearts and commitment of those in the pew and pulpit. I have seen many churches over time sabotage their future by clinging to the past rather than reaching for the future. Others sabotage their future by clinging to comfort and familiarity rather than moving into the unknown and facing challenges. As believers, we declare we are people of faith, but so often we choose familiarity rather than the future.

Below are the top ten practical hope builders that can improve many churches if taken seriously. I have listed them from the least important in most situations to the most important in terms of impact and moving a church forward. Consider and mark those that might be options for your church.

Top 10 Hope-Builders for Your Church
(Moving Forward in Faith and Function)

10. Update facilities to be comfortable, convenient, friendly to strangers, and attractive to your target audience.

9. Decentralize ministry throughout your city or region to make it more convenient, contextualized to target groups, and familiar.

8. Engage, as volunteers, established members in meaningful groups and places in the community and equip them to build relationships.

7. Use social media and other websites as invitational tools to outsiders, as well as insiders, designed to invite them into meaningful dialogue, relationships, partnerships, and/or ministry experiences.

6. Organize ministry staff, volunteer lay leaders, budget, and organization around mission functions rather than age groups or programming.

5. Provide ongoing opportunities for all persons to share their stories of how/when/where they encountered God at work and what that meant to them and others.

4. Create a way of measuring ministry effectiveness in keeping with an outward focus rather than just an inward focus of ministry and mission.

3. Empower and mobilize membership as priests in their families, communities, careers, and relationships.

2. Retool and reframe the mission of the church and role of pastor/staff to be sure these are built on biblical mandates of disciple making rather than on personal preferences or agenda.

1. Upgrade the role and function of greeters to include hospitality, welcoming, and engagement that invites others into the ministry design of the church.

Upgrade Greeters and
Create Invitational Culture

Part of recognizing that a body is in recovery means understanding that it cannot do everything at once. Let's begin with the something that is possible and can have significant results. Upgrade the role of greeters and improve your hospitality culture.

How does your church:

- Greet, welcome, assimilate, and engage guests?
- Invite guests into the missional experiences of your church?
- Help guests become engaged members?
- Create community among guests and newcomers and established members?
- Inform and invite guests and newcomers into an active life in church programming?

These critical questions can make or break a congregation's future. Without a clear, functional, simple, and intentional strategic response to each question, a church is likely to become or be experienced as ingrown, narcissistic, closed to outsiders, self-focused, and/or uncaring about making newcomers feel welcome and a part of church.

Experience and research indicate that unless a guest or newcomer meets and knows at least six persons by name and association (their family, school, neighborhood, and/or career) within six weeks, they are unlikely to become an active part of the congregation. How does this happen in your church? It doesn't usually just happen; it has to be planned for and the value lifted up in the church culture.

Often guests or newcomers feel lost, confused, unwanted, and alienated from the insider's language, the church's values, and historical traditions of the established congregation. Consider how clear these factors are to outsiders.

Answer each question "yes" or "no."

___ Do visitors know where to park in the parking lot?
___ Do newcomers know which door to enter?
___ Is signage in place to give directions, and are the signs in language and placement best for newcomers/guests?
___ Do you have greeters in the parking lot to welcome, direct, and provide assistance with children, umbrellas, etc., as needed and appropriate?
___ Are greeters in place to welcome guests at the entrance door?

___ Do they have name tags and a welcoming smile?

___ Do greeters know the church building layout, leadership, paths to the appropriate class for all newcomers?

___ Do those greeters introduce guests to persons of their same age as they make their way to the appropriate room for each member of the family?

___ Does the order of worship identify all in worship leadership by name and position?

___ Is your church language clear to outsiders–acrostics or acronyms on your website, newsletters, and worship folders–and inside words and jargon?

___ Is information readily available to describe the purpose/desired outcomes, target audience of each of the announced church activities? Is a process in place to invite guests to join church events?

___ Does the church provide a buddy for all newcomers/guests for six months to help them with questions, introductions to others, and onsite friends for their assimilation into the life of classes, church services, etc.?

___ Does someone invite newcomers immediately into music, worship, drama, mission activities, recreational experiences, or peer gatherings/fellowship?

___ Does someone invite them into possible leadership roles where they can shadow established leaders or maybe be part of a team of leaders who share their passion for issues of justice, the poor, or other missional endeavors?

___ Within a newcomer's first three months, do you offer an opportunity to sit down with a person gifted in spiritual discernment to explore the newcomer's gifting, calling, and desire/capacity to serve in and through the church?

___ Are newcomers invited immediately to join a designated social media page to build community and communication?

___ Do you invite newcomers to tour church facilities with a seasoned, informed, established church member who might share some history of the church as newcomers are introduced to various places in the facilities? (You might want to do this after a service and invite them to join you for a provided meal to continue the question-and-answer process and to build fellowship.)

___ Do you connect newcomers/guests with affinity groups within the membership that might provide networking, support in the workplace, family structures, sports, and/or communities? (Focus more on these affinity connections than traditional

Sunday school classes that so often are closed groups to most newcomers.)

___ Do you provide a four-to-five-week or five-hour newcomer orientation either in retreat setting or consecutive classes? (This is designed to provide relational experiences, basic information about who you are and who you are not as a church, something about basic organization, staffing, and opportunities for spiritual growth and mission.)

___ Do you explain what's available for children/youth and how they can best make these connections?

___ Do you provide a clear listing of opportunities and missional engagement of the congregation to give the big picture of how/when/where the church impacts and influences the community, state, and world?

What are three issues you are *not* doing well now that, if you improved or added, would significantly improve the culture of your church for guests and newcomers?

1. _____
2. _____
3. _____

An intentional, prayerful approach to upgrading greeters and welcoming services for guests and newcomers will certainly be deeply appreciated by newcomers and guests, but will also create a welcoming environment for all. If you fall into complacency and apathy regarding this critical issue, your church is certain to drift deeper into a maintenance mentality that turns you inward, rather than a missional mentality that pulls you outward so you might impact the world for the cause of Christ.

Working on assimilation and greeting issues is one sure step toward deeper hope and healthier relationships with persons inside and outside the congregational membership or attendees. The last section of this book offers many coaching tools designed to help you, your congregational leaders, and congregational coaches explore possibilities and challenges and establish some next steps in your process of recovering hope for your church.

PART IV

Sustaining Hope in Your Church

explores...

- Congregational Coaching: A Compass, Not a Map
- Signs of and Solutions for an Overprogrammed Church
- Rebooting Your Church–When? How?
- The Power of Focus, Prioritization, and Mobilization
- Making Events More Meaningful Experiences of Transformation
- How Churches Can Be Community without Becoming Cliques
- Ministering to Members on the Go

Hope in the Lord

Truly the eye of the Lord is on those who fear him,
   on those who hope in his steadfast love,

to deliver their soul from death,
   and to keep them alive in famine.

Our soul waits for the Lord;
   he is our help and shield.

Our heart is glad in him,
   because we trust in his holy name.

Let your steadfast love, O Lord, be upon us,
   even as we hope in you.

—Psalm 33:18–22, NRSV

16

Congregational Coaching

A COMPASS, NOT A MAP

"HOPE IS THE SHADOW OF FAITH."
—Austin O'Malley, *Keystones of Thought*

In health crisis and recovery, physicians practice medicine to find the most effective treatment to restore the patient to needed and desired health. As a patient in recovery, I was not sure I wanted them to practice on me! I wanted a sure and quick fix. After all, I had a lot I wanted to do, and I was tired of being sick! However, medical treatment is not always clear-cut. It often requires constant assessment, monitoring, and adjusting of treatment to discover what is best for each individual case.

Churches in recovery are much the same. The congregational coaching approach is not a quick fix, it is not a clear map; but it does provide a compass for a church to move forward in more healthy and productive directions. The realities are challenging and call for great patience, prayer, and perseverance if health will have a chance to return to the body.

Many congregations are adrift in a sea of challenges—opportunities against the winds of increasing secularity, diminishing interest in church attendance, diversity of people groups, and personal preferences. Such challenges provide fertile soil for coaching. Congregational coaching is about focus, discovering priorities, deepening learnings, and strengthening leaders to carry out discerned ministry goals to move the congregation forward in faith and function.

Coaching provides tools, questions, and deep listening. The well-trained coach not only listens *to* the congregation but *for* the congregation. These skills and tools help a congregation bring an issue to the surface and focus on priorities from the collective voices in the process. The processes selected by the coach and staff are critical and must be aligned with the learning styles of those involved. Coaching is about deepening and broadening vision and the leadership pool for a more effective ministry. The coach begins with staff, then key leaders (as defined by the church), moving deeper into the congregation and engaging them in interviews among the community. The development of prayer triads, sermons, testimonials, and reflection provides the framework for the Spirit to move. The coach's job is to create the safe and open place for deep, focused, and forward-thinking conversations that become the framework/direction for the next three-to-five years of ministry.

What Is Congregational Coaching?

Congregational coaching is a collaborative, intentional, co-created process that empowers pastor, staff, key leaders, and congregation to discover and embrace God's future for their local congregation. The coach approach is not about giving answers as much as it is a strategy that provides processes for you to find answers as the coach asks powerful questions, explores options and challenges, and finds and takes next steps to move you forward in ministry.

Coaching is all about finding and maintaining focus and momentum that move you forward in effectiveness and function. In a time of rapidly changing and diverse culture, finding and keeping focus and maximizing time and resources are keys for forward movement of a church. A trained congregational coach provides:

- An open, safe, and discerning atmosphere that ensures a place for all voices in the conversation to be heard
- A listening heart and ear that strive deeply to hear the Spirit's leadership, the energy in the room, and those in the mix of the conversation
- A safe and guided space that encourages intergenerational conversations designed to explore, encourage, challenge, clarify, and prioritize next steps
- Prayerful dialogue to discover potential roadblocks to progress and solutions for moving forward now
- Space and guidance for the group to craft a time line for implementing the strategy they have discerned

- A clarifying, humorous perspective amid tense situations
- Opportunities for celebrating God's movement in the congregation's midst and the future God presents to the body of Christ

The coach approach to strategic planning with congregations is a collaborative effort for spiritually discerning the focus for a congregation for the next three-to-five years. The process includes prayer triads with members, interviews with the pastor and staff, coaching key leaders, and working with the congregation as they seek to discover common threads and to discern gaps and challenges as well as opportunities. Part of this often leads the congregation to do some interviews with community leaders, organizations, and other churches to seek out affirmations or challenges as well as possible partnerships.

Once this information is gathered and prioritized by the leaders and the congregation, if there's alignment and positive energy, the group decides on next steps. If disconnects or stress surfaces, the coach begins to "drill down" to get clarity and consensus on "where to go from here." If the congregation asks for the coach's opinion, most coaches will share their opinions, but the primary covenant between a coach and a congregation is that the coach works from their agenda, keeping his/her personal agenda neutral and out of the outcome. The outcome is that discovered and embraced by the congregation and not that prescribed or recommended by the coach. Such a process provides many positive contributions to a congregational strategy plan. The congregational coach approach:

- Provides a collaborative process that invites and encourages a breadth of diverse voices in the process.
- Works best in healthy congregations.
- Is forward focused and rarely works on issues from the past.
- Can unlock the "lies that bind" and distract some congregations.
- Is action oriented and does not get bogged down in "just conversation."
- Is an intentional framing of agreed-upon next steps.
- Provides a tool for dealing with church bullies that often control church direction.
- Creates a deepening of commitment to new dreams and action plans.
- Broadens the leadership base and ownership of next steps.
- Is based on spiritual discernment, alignment of actions with core values, and consensus.

- Reenergizes floundering, healthy congregations trapped in maintenance and survival loops of beliefs and behaviors.

CONGREGATIONAL COACHING...

- Is more about the depth of listening than the depth of knowledge of the coach.
- Is about designing a collaborative process that discerns God's leadership.
- Is about deepening the fellowship, prayer, and dialogue among members, leaders, and staff.
- Is about opening possibilities that will move the leaders and congregation forward.
- Empowers lay leaders to have a voice in discovering, discerning, prioritizing, and implementing next steps.
- Deepens ownership and leadership for new dreams and visions.
- Is about discovering the gaps in values, thinking, alignment, or behaviors and/or beliefs.
- Creates missional momentum and metrics.
- Is about "showing up" and being "fully present" in congregational dialogues
- Is about nurturing hope and dreams while affirming and celebrating forward movement in faith and function.

WHAT IS THE COACH'S FUNCTION/ROLE?

The role of a coach is different from that of a traditional consultant. Coaches listen deeply to what is being said and what is not being said to determine connections and disconnects between dreams, desires, faith, and organizational infrastructure. Coaches pay attention to the movement of the Spirit amid conversations with staff, key leaders, congregation, community leaders, and persons inside and outside leadership circles.

The coach's role is not to bring a prescription to fix problems as much as the coach brings a process designed to invite as many voices as possible into a discernment process of what God desires for the church now, and how to live into that vision and calling. The coach leads the congregation to listen to one another across generational lines, classes, groups of persons who are in the established church, and those who might be new to the fellowship or visiting the fellowship. Ultimately the coach is to keep the group moving forward in faith and action to find and experience the next level in ministry.

Clarifying Distinctions between Functions

CONSULTANT	FACILITATOR	CONGREGATIONAL COACH
Provides a prescription to resolve problems	Offers guiding presence	Provides deep listening and coaching presence
Brings expertise and experience to the situation	Negotiates through challenges	Provides powerful questions to unlock discovery and action
Engaged to fix the problems	Engaged to move the conversation	Engaged to work with coachable persons to explore options, possibilities, and create an action plan
Identifies challenges and barriers	Creates a conversation to address challenges and barriers	Moves the group, through collaboration exercises, to find and take next steps

WHAT ARE A COACH'S DESIRED OUTCOMES?

Coaches work to achieve the desired outcomes of the person/ congregation for whom they are working. Desired outcomes come from the client–the church or group in the church that actually contracts with the coach to move them forward.

Having contracted with a client, a coach's primary function early on is to get clear about their desired outcomes and the readiness and coachability of at least the pastor/staff and key leaders. The coach wants to work in a culture that is open to forward movement, desires to connect with the Spirit's leadership, and is open to any change/transition they feel God is leading them to and through. Without these elements the best coach can have a bad coaching experience, and the congregation will be disappointed when many of them might be looking for quick fixes rather than engaging in a discovery process to move them to deeper depths and higher heights of the love of God.

What People Are Saying about Congregational Coaching

The coach approach to strategic planning is a collaborative effort designed to help congregations discover and take the best steps to move the church forward in faith and function, not necessarily to find consensus that keeps everyone happy. The coach is able, as an objective outsider, without a "dog in the fight," to listen carefully, paying careful attention, without judgment, to what is happening (and not happening) among the pastor/staff, key leaders, congregation, and community. After working with more than one hundred churches of various denominations, I have received many comments from pastors and key leaders after they have experienced all or a portion of the coach approach to strategic planning. Here are some of those comments:

Randy McKinney, pastor of Longview Church in Raleigh, North Carolina, declared, after five months of coaching with me, "Congregational coaching is more like a compass than a map." Randy gave me a great descriptor and metaphor for coaching in congregational settings.

———— •◆• ————

Clergy and lay leaders who have been involved in congregational coaching experiences have made statements such as:

> "A powerful experience that lets every voice be heard and provides powerful questions that build bridges instead of barriers as we face multiple challenges as a congregation."
>
> "A fun-filled, authentic time of spiritual conversations designed to hear deeply the voice of God and the voices of all age groups of those in the church and outside the church. The process is always forward moving and prevents us from replaying challenges of the past, but helps us learn from successes and failures from our past."
>
> "The coach engages the group, keeps us focused without giving his/her opinion, unless asked for from the group. The coach asks powerful questions rather than giving advice!"
>
> "Our congregational coaching sessions were all about discovering options, possibilities! We also explored possible barriers and solutions to those barriers to keep us moving. Coaching created a real 'pull' for our church rather than feeling we were being 'pushed' to do something we do not want to do."
>
> "I just loved the coaching process. We talked about issues we have needed to talk about for a long time but were too busy (or in some cases too scared) to engage in the conversations. The coach created an atmosphere and process that served us well!"

———— •◆• ————

Review these quotes from pastors and congregations that have experienced the three-to-five-month process of "Finding and Embracing Their Future: A Coach Approach to Strategy Planning":

"The spirit around here is very good. A lot of positive ministry ideas are not only bubbling up but also being implemented. We had a couple of young couples join the church last Sunday, and one of them had pretty much been in the 70 percent. We reached them through a young adult Bible study group that meets on Wednesday night. We're also having more guests in worship who are actually looking for a church home, something we've not had in a long, long time. Most of them are newcomers. Worship attendance is up, and we have a much better spirit. People are engaging with each other and with guests after worship."

—R. Prince, after our first session

"The three-step process of orientation/reality check, assessment/discovery, and interpreting data/discernment worked well. The openness of the process as well as the adaptability to our context was refreshing. While a step-by-step guide would have alleviated some fear for the majority of leaders, I appreciated the way the method employed by Eddie stretched us beyond our comfort zones and linear ways of thinking.

"The most helpful part of the process was the face-to-face encounters we had with Eddie. His coaching allowed us to have some open and honest conversations. Likewise, the sense of direction that we now have is extremely helpful as we begin to more fully embrace the call to be the presence of Christ beyond the four walls of the building."

—Randy McKinney, Pastor, Longview Baptist,
Raleigh, North Carolina

"As a result of our congregational coaching with Eddie, we have experienced tremendous missional movement in touching our immediate community for Christ and, specifically, using the apartments that our church acquired in 2007 as a hub of ministry targeting the working poor, college students, and senior adults to meet educational, vocational, medical, and spiritual needs. Ministries such as work with the unsheltered homeless, a monthly medical clinic, an after-school program for children, college student work, a community garden, and the hiring of an Oakmont Community Center Minister who lives in the apartments are among a few examples that have emerged and/or been enhanced as a result of Eddie's coaching and from the influence of our weekly spiritual formation groups at Oakmont."

—Dr. Greg Rogers, Pastor, Oakmont Baptist Church,
Greenville, North Carolina

"First, I would like to offer my thanks for your guidance, your candor, and your expertise as Longview completes this discernment process in the coming weeks. One thing that has become clear to (most) all of the folks who have participated in the visioning sessions with you is the difference between a consultant and a coach!! :)

"I have been doing some thinking as to what this has meant to me over the past couple of months. Although I haven't been able to participate in every action that has been recommended to complete the process, it has been very thought provoking and really paradigm shifting in how I have thought about 'church.' I guess that's the real objective, to shake 'conventional' beliefs and notions to the core in order to reshape the mold of how our church interacts with those in the church community—those who live in the same physical vicinity as the church location, those who church members interact with on a regular basis, AND those who church members may simply encounter intentionally or unintentionally. The key result of this to me has been the idea of expanding Longview's sphere of influence through utilizing the conventional 'strengths' we have but also realizing that culture today (use of social media, busy lifestyles, falling 'regular' churchgoers) will make it hard for our church to grow in huge numbers (and also this really shouldn't be our metric of church 'success') but presents huge opportunities to develop an expanded sphere of influence. These opportunities—and new methods of interaction—must be embraced because change is REAL, it's HERE, and it ain't going back to the 1960s, as some undoubtedly would like to see. Only those churches that embrace the opportunities given by the brave new world of 2011—and the future—cultural mores are going to thrive in what our ultimate goal should be...simply, to have as much influence as we can in bringing people to a closer relationship to Jesus Christ. We must realize that, as much as we would like new members to fill our pews and our coffers, future 'success' for Longview won't be measured in the number of people who are members of our church, but will be measured in far less quantitative and definitive metrics."

—Josh Spencer, Deacon

"The greatest contributions of our coaching process were that it helped us focus on our future instead of our divided past. It gave us three important priorities on which our highly diverse congregation could agree to focus. At the beginning of the process, we were healing from a church split. Many in our congregation thought we needed to discern the problems that caused people to leave and fix those problems. Furthermore, our church members were pulling in different directions and advocating many different priorities.

"Through our coaching process we identified many possible priorities. Before we began our coaching process, we had a considerable amount of skepticism from some members about the coaching process. They believed it was like a consultative process in which someone would come in, identify our problems, and propose changes. After that, we would promptly shelve the proposed changes. But the coaching process was different in that while we got a lot of good direction from Eddie, he led us to diagnose problems ourselves and come up with our own proposed changes. He would tell us what he thought when we asked him to, but he didn't push his opinions. We were able to develop a consensus on three issues that were most important.

—Robert Prince, Pastor, First Baptist Church,
Waynesville, North Carolina

Other stories from churches engaged in the congregational coaching process celebrate shifts, advancements, and changes in behaviors and attitudes. What celebrations speak to you the most? Which shifts are most needed in your church now?

Stories of Celebration

Rev. Ginger Isom, pastor of a United Methodist church in Greeneville, Tennessee, celebrates a variety of new partnerships with community agencies and congregations to help her small congregation deepen their impact and influence in the community. An online radio talk show, a community garden, and a host of mobilized lay leaders have been developed in the last two years!

"Drag" Kimrey, Congregational Coach, Interim Pastor, and Elder at *Midway Presbyterian Church*, Maxton, North Carolina (small rural struggling congregation with about 30 in average attendance), speaking of the congregation's progress on goals clarified through the coaching process, the elder testified:

"Just some comments about last night and last Sunday's Congregational meeting. If you missed last night, you missed an absolutely fantastic Bible study night and discussion. We had a little smaller crowd due to previous commitments, but the discipleship topic of the DVD and the subsequent discussions (including our visitors) were simply outstanding. We are gaining spiritual momentum with every session. I love it!! Great job, Julia!!!!!! It excites me to see how you have embraced this concept and how dedicated you are to growing and improving it. As far as Sunday night goes, I was just blown away by what came out of this meeting and how excited everyone was (especially the congregation). GOD is in this, folks!! When we started, I felt like we were nine people in a life boat that was taking water slowly (we were bailing hard to stay afloat). Now, I feel like we are on board a cruise ship with 30+ people headed to destination unknown, but excited and looking forward to the journey!!!!! I was excited about this from the beginning, now I'm off the charts!!!!!!! 'THANK YOU' from the bottom of my heart for your dedication, hard work, commitment, passion, excitement, and love for your church and this process. We serve an awesome GOD who loves you. I love you, too."

Endorsement by *Midway Presbyterian Church's* Congregational Coach:

"Recently I completed the requirements for certification as a congregational coach. I was Supply Pastor for a small Presbyterian church in rural Robeson County, N.C. To satisfy the requirements for certification, I employed recently-learned skills that helped this congregation to begin to answer the question they posed to me at my interview with the Session, "What do we have to do to grow?" At the time of the interview I had no idea. This was a small church in the middle of nowhere. How could it grow? I was thinking the same as they: growth meant numerical growth; more people to help pay the bills.

"Today, after leading this congregation through congregational coaching, I now know that the expected demise of such a congregation has been put on hold and may even have been fully eliminated. The congregational coaching process has brought forth a new energy among the people. The congregational coaching process has identified that numerical growth must first begin with congregational spiritual growth. The congregational coaching process has shown that the congregation moves forward into the future using the power of its identified strengths and not dwelling on its weaknesses or poor demographic situation.

"I believe that congregational coaching is an appropriate process for the whole congregation and certainly meaningful for smaller groups within the congregation."

–L.D. "Drag" Kimrey, D.Min.

———— •◆• ————

"I have been coaching congregational leaders for almost ten years. I have seen, and personally experienced, the difference coaching can make in a leader's life and ministry. It was a natural next step to take congregational coach training. It has enhanced my coaching skills, broadened my sphere of influence, and enabled me to help congregations move forward. I saw positive results with the first congregation I coached using the process taught by Eddie Hammett. The congregation was able to openly deal with some of the issues that were holding them back, and to make Spirit-inspired decisions about their future. The coaching process empowered the congregation to be pro-active in their own ministry instead of passively allowing the pastor and session to make all the ministry decisions."

–Dr. Peggy Hinds, Mid-Kentucky Presbytery

Mitch Coggins, Congregational Coach at *Eastminster Presbyterian Church*, Indiana, reports on the take aways from a coaching session at the church:

- My priorities are echoed by many. Time management is a challenge during the process.
- Promise, hope, vision have come a step closer. Teamwork is stronger. We are in this to achieve the will of God—and to discern where He is leading us. Exciting!
- Good process. Interesting the amount of agreement. Willingness to discuss difficult topics speaks well for the process.
- Very enlightening. I had no idea how much the church really did need help, or how much the pastor was actually doing for the church.
- Happy with support from those who gave up a day to be here. Worried at the prospect of introducing an entertainment factor into service. Interested to hear thoughts of others.
- Good format. Appreciate what we have—hope we can keep it.
- Good process of getting us to think about goals and priorities of future planning for EPC.
- Good presentation with ideas and plans for the future.
- Generally good process. Time allotted to meeting might be increased (lot to cover in time-frame)
- Much more awareness. Areas we had not given much thought to. Great to have many opinions.
- Different ways to look at things. Good meeting.

- I thought the session went well. Enjoyed hearing other people's ideas. I think it is a great idea to involve the entire church in the "brainstorming" process.
- Good process. Good give and take. Much clarification needed.
- Set up with table leaders (excellent). We all had ideas, suggestions. We see all as dedicated individuals who will serve God in the best way and draw more people to church.
- Good opportunity to express my ideas and perceive the ideas (feelings) of others on what we need to do for our church.
- Very touching to experience the sincerity of those in the room. Thoughtful, incisive discussions.
- Seems there is a lot to contemplate. Some problems can be easily solved, some will take time.
- Budget issues are important to most of the big problems, and we didn't address that at all. Some people who were asked to attend are not always ready to solve problems.
- Concerned that priorities are too specific.
- Loved process & felt it was good and honest discussion. Large group ideas flowed back and forth easily, helping me look behind the eyes of others and think about things my brain hadn't even conceived.
- I thought it was productive. A little rough starting in terms of processing information, but the energy in the room was great! I thought. I'm very optimistic. Nice job, Carrie and Mitch. In summary, I:
  1. learned a lot about our church;
  2. gained appreciation for the problems we need to solve;
  3. realized that intractable changes loom on the horizon that need to be anticipated.
- The greatest contributions of our coaching process were that it helped us focus on our future instead of our divided past, and it gave us three important priorities on which our highly diverse congregation could agree to focus. At the beginning of the process, we were healing from a church split, and many in our congregation thought we needed to discern the problems that caused people to leave and fix those problems. Furthermore, our church members were pulling in different directions and advocating many different priorities.

First Baptist Church, Kernersville, North Carolina, celebrates clarifying focus of priorities, mobilizing lay leaders in worship planning and services, updating the children's department, and engaging Hispanic children in Bible study opportunities. They are also celebrating a community garden and engaging the community through these options.

Oakmont Baptist Church, Greenville, North Carolina, found focus through their efforts in spiritual formation, clarifying next steps, and purchasing and renovating local apartments for community ministry options connecting a variety of people and age groups.

Wake Forest Baptist Church, Wake Forest, North Carolina, processed options for their land-locked historic church facing high growth in limited space. They decided on priorities, realigned staff, built relationships with the local seminary, and miraculously were given permission to purchase land to build needed space.

First Baptist Church, Tucker, Georgia, turned their focus from inward, "come structures and metrics" to outward-focused, "go structures and metrics." The twenty-somethings launched a small group and a Friday night gathering on the Main Street lawn to attract others in their downtown location. They are deepening their investment in their local schools and transitioning community. They also are learning to build meaningful relationships with neighbors, community agencies, and their onsite Network and Child Development Centers. A great lab for churches facing transition with courage, faith, and innovation!

Longview Baptist Church, Raleigh, North Carolina, continues to embrace their new pastor. Clarity of focus empowered them to rethink and redesign their worship space to attract and minister more effectively to younger families.

First Baptist Church, Lumberton, North Carolina, found focus and momentum that caused them to give their church a long overdue facelift inside and out. Laypersons rallied to the cause and made it happen. They continue to deepen their impact among special folks and their families as they extend their missional ministries in their city and beyond through hands-on ministry opportunities with the homeless and persons of all ages.

First Baptist Church, Waynesboro, Virginia, faced the challenge of two worship services, intergenerational concerns, and challenges of "becoming two churches" with courage and prayer. Their focusing efforts allowed folks from many different perspectives to have their voices heard, and coaching created space for alignment of feelings, facts, and future potential.

Hayes Barton Baptist Church, Raleigh, North Carolina, is a traditional congregation seeking to reach a changing community filled with adults of all ages, values, and belief systems. They not only found focus in priorities, but new leadership teams emerged to carry out next steps. Differing perspectives and values emerged, but found increased understanding and clarity that created new momentum for new outreach strategies to professionals and artists in their community.

———— •◆• ————

Often I hear lay leaders and congregational members of all ages say, "I really never thought about this issue the way that person (another person outside their inner circle or age group) thinks about it." The coach approach often puts people of different age groups, careers, and socioeconomic conditions in groups to discuss their perspectives on priorities that emerge through prayer, reflection, and dialogue.

Other times I hear congregational members declare, "Wow, we are doing much more than I ever realized!" The process is designed to give individuals, small table groups, leadership teams, and congregational members or guests opportunities to hear from one another all the things God is doing now, not to mention the dreams/ visions they have about what God is calling them to in the future. It creates super new friendships and internal momentum and hope!

I have also heard people in a congregation discover some clarity about disconnects that are identified by the group. This epiphany is often expressed by words like these: "Well, that explains a lot for me!" "That makes sense now that I know why." These are the words and experiences coaches live for and certainly celebrate!

While many stories of celebration are directly connected to congregational coaching, challenges and steep learning curves also emerge that take more time, energy, and intentionality. A major issue that often surfaces deals with the overprogrammed church designed for a church culture and an age when there were not dual-career marriages, single-parent homes, and competition with community and career events and expectations.

17

Signs of and Solutions for an Overprogrammed Church

FROM LEADER FATIGUE TO LEADER FULFILLMENT

> "HOPE SIMPLY DEALS WITH POSSIBILITIES.
> IF SOMETHING IS STILL POSSIBLE—EVEN IN OUR WILDEST DREAMS—
> IF THERE IS STILL A GLIMMER OF HOPE,
> IT IS WORTH HANGING ON TO FOR AS LONG AS IT EXISTS."
> —Peter G. Doumit, *What I Know about Baseball Is What I Know about Life*

As I entered a rehabilitation process after my heart surgery, I learned pretty quickly that recovery was all of a sudden my full-time job—my priority and focus of time, energy, and resources. Did I have other things I needed to do and wanted to do? Yes! But I quickly realized I had no choice but to focus on recovery to ensure my health stabilized so I could go back to work and live a productive life.

I'm writing this book almost six years after this health crisis began. I'm feeling better than I ever have in my life. Occasionally, I am reminded by rapid heartbeats or atrial flutters that I'm still a heart patient and that I still have some health to be restored; but I'm healthy and enjoying life and ministry once again! I'm grateful to God and blatantly aware of the journey I have been on. To be honest, I would repeat it all again to be as clear and focused and healthy as I am today.

The journey has been deeply transforming for me. Yes, it has been tough and challenging, but God has brought me to–and He is bringing me through–the challenge. My faith is deeper than ever. My appreciation for every breath and heartbeat is real and constant. My gratitude for others–my physicians, therapist, and care-givers–is genuine and deep. You cannot go through such a health crisis alone. We must be willing to reach out and receive help from others. This was not easy at all for me–a very independent, self-sufficient man. The challenge is no less for the body of Christ in the midst of recovery.

As a church and clergy coach, I frequently hear pastors and other church leaders declare:

"We cannot find enough leaders."

"Our people are just not faithful and committed enough."

"Our members ask, 'What is the church going to do for me?' rather than asking, 'What can I do for the church?'"

"Our members take positions, but they do not lead and have to be pushed, prodded, and persuaded to get the job done."

"Our leaders are tired; they are busy people and do not have much time for church responsibilities."

"We have good people, loving people, nice people; but they like to be served rather than to serve others."

These statements of frustration are often signs of an overprogrammed church, leader fatigue, and loss of fulfillment in serving. The self-test/assessment below provides a tool to help you self-assess your situation. I suggest that each pastor/staff and key leader take this assessment individually and then compile your responses. Then invite the congregation to complete the inventory. Compare all responses. Dialogue about discoveries and solutions. Consider...

- What similarities and differences are evident between pastor/staff and volunteer leaders?
- What patterns are present among various age groups taking the assessment?
- What are the top five issues from all responses?
- What is the accumulated score for the church (including responses from pastors, staff, and congregational members and leaders)?

Is Your Church Overprogrammed?
(A Self-test to Determine If It's Tme to Get Out the Pruning Shears)

Position in the church: (circle response)

    pastor/staff   volunteer   leader   member   guest

Age of person responding: (circle range)

    15–20   21–40   41–55   56–70   71–up

Years Involved in this church:

    Under 5   5–10   11–15   16–25   26+

Instructions: Respond honestly to each question by circling one answer. Tally your responses at the bottom.

Self-Assessment Inventory of Church Programming

1.	Does your church face an annual struggle to fill all the teacher/worker positions in your educational program?	YES	NO
2.	Each year, several people are asked to serve because jobs need to be done rather than because people want to do that ministry.	YES	NO
3.	Do you have two or more programs or ministries serving similar purposes that compete for participants or leaders?	YES	NO
4.	Does it take 75 percent or more of your available adult workers to fully staff the ministries within the walls of the church so that fewer than 25 percent of your people are investing themselves in ministries outside the church walls?	YES	NO
5.	Does your church have meetings, services, or programs that people attend more from habit or duty than because they are life-giving? (Clue: Do the regulars complain about the lack of commitment of those who do not attend?)	YES	NO
6.	Are leaders, other than paid staff, allowed or encouraged to take on more than two ongoing ministry responsibilities, one major and one minor?	YES	NO
7.	Has some major new ministry stalled in its development for lack of workers?	YES	NO
8.	Have you recently overheard lay leaders say that church meetings and responsibilities are taking more time than they wished?	YES	NO
9.	Do you have ministry programs in which it is easier to fill "rank and file" spots than to fill key leadership roles?	YES	NO
10.	Do you often see signs of worker burnout—people feeling overworked, resigning ministry positions earlier than they had planned to, or saying they need to take a break from ministry?	YES	NO

Total Responses: YES_____ NO_____

BONUS QUESTIONS

1.	Does your church have a system in place to equip every present and new member to identify spiritual gifts and personal calling and then to help each one connect with a ministry that matches that call?	YES	NO
2.	Does your church encourage and support the birthing of new ministries when members identify calls to ministries not yet in existence?	YES	NO
3.	In the past year, have you witnessed the birth of at least one new ministry that was not started by a church board or committee but by a member in response to vision God gave him or her?	YES	NO
4.	In the past year, has your church deliberately ended at least one ministry program or regular meeting?	YES	NO
5.	Has your church set a goal to have half of all adult members involved in ministries outside the walls of the church?	YES	NO

Total Responses: YES_____   NO_____

SCORING

Give your church 10 points for each yes in response to questions 1 through 10. Now subtract 20 points for each yes in response to bonus questions 1 through 5.

MY SCORE: _____

negative 100–0   Wow! A truly empowered church
10–30   On track but could do better
40–60   Time to get the pruning shears
70–100   You need to clarify your church's ministry vision before you'll know where to prune.

MY NEXT STEPS WILL BE

1. _____
2. _____
3. _____
4. _____

After doing your assessment and comparing it to the response of other leaders, staff, congregation, and guests, ask yourself:

1. What are our learnings from this inventory?
2. What are the possibilities for addressing our discoveries?
3. Which three ideas that surfaced could help us most now?
4. What could prevent us moving forward?
5. Who can help us make these needed shifts?

Making needed shifts in values, structures, and behaviors is best done from the inside out; that is, internal emotions, valued traditions, family history/heritage often drive what is done and not done. The basic rule of thumb for introducing and managing any change and transition is to change personal preference values *before* you try to change structures/organizations. Learning to live into your church's core values and being open to new expressions of these core values is critical. The coach approach to change is explained in *Making Shifts without Making Waves: A Coach Approach to Soulful Leadership* by Hammett and Pierce, www.transformingsolutions.org.

Often a direct correlation exists among an overprogrammed church, leader fatigue, deteriorating commitment, and involvement in congregational life. Facing the reality rather than blaming the leaders is critical to moving forward and reawakening the passion and calling to serve.

Getting a Handle on Leader Fatigue

Overprogrammed churches fuel leader fatigue that frequently leads to leader burnout. Left unaddressed, leader fatigue will evolve into leader burnout and lead to a deficit of leaders or, worse yet, bitter leaders.

Leader fatigue seems to be growing and challenges many pastors, staff, and congregations who are organized around multiple ministries designed for every age group. This is particularly true in a small- or medium-size church that feels compelled to compete with the larger churches in town. Smaller congregations cannot offer a wealth of programs; they can offer selective programming and build partnerships and alliances for other services/ministries.

More often than not, most congregations thirty years or older are inward focused–taking care of "us" (those in the flock). The inward-focused value system grows as membership dwindles or grows into complacency and apathy. When congregational care becomes *the* primary value system of those in the pew, and often those in the pulpit, the organizational culture generates fuel for leader fatigue. The self-care and maintenance mentality not only generates an inward-focused congregation, but often an overprogrammed church. An overprogrammed church keeps creating programs to serve those on the inside, with little regard for reaching those on the outside. The congregation begins to plateau in attendance, and commitment diminishes.

Energy of leaders begins to erode as programs increase to reach growing demands of the self-focused membership. Programs increase but leaders do not. The vision is to sustain what is, rather than move to the next level in the mission and calling of the church. Eventually the faithful leaders become fatigued and begin to fall away. Spiritual formation for leaders gives way to busyness to keep the church programs running and to keep members happy. Faithfulness becomes more about keeping things the same in the church rather than aligning members' lives to the call of Christ. So leaders not only experience a spiritual deficit that fuels fatigue, but also they give and give and never find themselves in places to receive and embrace the presence of Christ in their lives.

Invite leaders into an honest, nonconfrontational, nonblaming dialogue. Ask for feedback and suggestions rather than assuming or blaming. Consider these powerful coaching questions:

1. What is missing for you?
2. What would make our ministry more fulfilling and effective?
3. What have you wanted to say about church but no one asked or listened?
4. What needs to happen here to make service meaningful for you?
5. What programs are devouring too much of your time?
6. What energizes you?
7. What is God calling you to be/do now?

Signs of an Overprogrammed Church

While an overprogrammed church and leader fatigue manifest themselves differently in different types of churches, this self-assessment tool might help you begin a dialogue. More often than not, overprogrammed churches...

- Have a calendar of events each day of the week with no consistent "white space" protected for reflection, family time, or community engagement.
- Protect their programs rather than being intentional and concerned about penetrating their community and culture for Christ.
- Defend budget percentages that reflect spending more on *us* (the members) than on reaching *them* (those beyond the active membership) when the percentages of unchurched far outnumber the membership in our churches.
- Value busyness of church activity rather than the business of joining God's mission in the world.
- Focus conversations, strategies, and planning of staff and ministry teams more on "what's good for our members" rather than "what will serve our community beyond membership and those with no expressed interest in faith."
- Expend massive amounts of energy, time, and money debating issues that have little significance in the kingdom

of God (eg., debates on times, schedules, clothes, worship styles, music, color of carpet, etc.).

Facing the realities of church life takes courage, faith, and willingness to move beyond preferences and perceptions to realties that can move you forward in faith and function. This is often a tough and risky road for pastors/staff and key leaders. The vocal minority often chooses not to face reality; they would rather live in dysfunction or denial or both. Often these vocal members are not actively involved in building the church. Rather they are responsible, at least in part, for keeping the church stuck and in denial about reality. For a church to move forward, fatigued leaders must become empowered and fulfilled leaders who have caught a God-sized vision for moving the church into the future.

Moving from Leader Fatigue to Leader Fulfillment and Impact

What moves a church suffering from leader fatigue to a church of empowered leaders who impact the world for Christ? There is hope! The shift begins with leaders who have a shift of heart, values, and a commitment to redefining the way they spend their time, energy, and money. This might begin with just pastor/staff; it might include the deacon and/or elders, or it might be one or two leaders of influence who are willing to shift their ministries. By validating this new remnant of leaders, expressing and living by different values, a church can dig out a new path, and a new role model for leadership can emerge. As these leaders tap into God's callings on their lives and their spiritual gifts, excitement brews, passion grows, and impact is experienced by all touched and involved.

Possible Solutions for an Overprogrammed Church and Leader Fatigue

- Reallocate energy, resources, and time around what is moving the church forward in its divine mission.
- Provide required and resourced annual refueling opportunities for pastor/staff and leaders that renew their spirit, keeping their vision fresh and their skills sharp.
- Be intentional about providing sabbaticals for pastor/staff and all key volunteer leaders after five consistent years of service. This should include rest away from ministry roles, spiritual nourishment, and next-level training (equipping them for future ministry needs). The entire church should affirm, resource, and encourage this time of leader refreshment.

- Sponsor an inventory and dialogue every two years to discover "what's working," "what's not working," and "what's next" to keep the church aligned with God's divine mission.
- Establish criteria for deleting/adding programs, and use these to assess the situation every three years. Such criteria need to be prayed about and prepared by key leaders who are passionate about the church's present and future mission.
- Add a unit of ministry in programming for every additional thirty members/guests.
- Delete two units of ministry (committees, classes, groups) for every thirty persons the church loses without replacing them.
- Add an additional paid staff member for every one hundred new members reached to ensure numerical growth of membership.
- Evaluate staffing each time the church loses one hundred people.
- Develop programs from passion of members rather than from dictates of staff or denomination.
- Create partnerships and alliances with other churches, community groups, and gifted leaders to increase offerings, deepen excellence of service, and strengthen community goals.
- Consider a collaborative agreement between churches and groups to provide the resources for a church, cluster of churches, or community. In the new economy new staffing models are emerging for multisite and multicareer pastors/staffs. Explore, take some risks, and spread your leadership base instead of layering more tasks on fewer leaders.[1]
- Provide external and internal coaches to grow leaders forward in capacity, skill sets, and vision.
- Encourage and face with courage learning curves and assist with aligning resources.[2]
- Provide a congregational coach in residence to nurture vision, guide projects, grow leaders, and serve as transition from one staffing arrangement to another staffing arrangement.[3]

Sometimes the new awareness of the challenges generates needs for deeper understandings and exploring possibilities for "rebooting your system" of church programs and ministry design to design a program that is more relevant for your church today.

18

Rebooting Your
Church—When? How?

"THE DEEPEST DARK REVEALS THE STARRIEST HOPE."
—Gerald Massey, "Long Expected"

Life is different for me now. I have a different focus for life and sustaining health. My attitudes and behaviors have shifted to healthier options. My priorities for time, energy, and resources have shifted significantly to ensure my health improves. I have rebooted my life in light of the health crisis I am living and growing through.

Churches are no different as they pursue health and recovery. Church is challenging at best on so many fronts these days. The growing diversity of our population, the 24–7 world that impacts family life, social life, work life, and now church life seems to be creating a yearning and growing need to learn how to reboot our church programming. How might we know when rebooting of programming is called for? What might rebooting a church look like? How can we then reboot without creating unnecessary conflict, polarization, or diminished interest?

Assessing the Need to
Reboot Church Programming

After working in church and denominational leadership for thirty years and coaching and consulting pastors and other leaders for ten years, I believe that most churches are struggling at some level with effectiveness. Some are experimenting with a variety of different strategies, with varying degrees of success. Many churches are fearful of trying anything new or different in their context for fear of rocking the boat and possibly losing contributing members.

Such fear causes churches just to rock on and pray things get better as they encourage and sometimes use guilt to get people to participate in leadership and to attend programs and events simply to keep church programs alive. How might a church know when rebooting is being called for in their context?

Consider which of these are evident now in your church:

- Dwindling attendance in one or more programs over a six-to-twelve-month period;
- Increasing difficulty in enlisting dependable and competent leaders to staff existing programs;
- Diminished motivation among current leaders, as evidenced by low morale, lack of preparation, and/or inconsistency in program leadership.
- Spiritually depleted leaders, as evidenced by unmet spiritual thirsts or challenges;
- A growing void of available and willing leaders for the hosts of existing volunteer positions needed;
- Insufficient financial resources to provide adequately for all traditional programming;
- Overprogrammed leaders and staff who feel stretched beyond their limits, or feel they are just going through the motions without much passion or results;
- Discouraged leaders and participants;
- Members faithful to church programs to preserve history, community image, or personal preference rather than being faithful to fulfilling God's mission;
- Hunger among core key leaders and a remnant of members to improve effectiveness, efficiency, and faithfulness to God's mission;
- People becoming open to explore options and to try something new;
- People becoming willing to take risks and to walk into fear to be more fruitful, less frustrated.

What Rebooting a Church
Looks Like in Your Context

Rebooting is a fairly familiar computer term. Sometimes when computers get stuck, freeze up, and are unable to function properly, the entire system has to be turned off and rebooted by resetting the system. What might rebooting look like in your context? Context is important in today's world. Churches, communities, leaders, and resources are often different just a few miles down the road. So getting at this, the coach approach offers tools for discerning, exploring, discovering, and moving collaboratively into new dreams and visions. How might a group of key leaders begin to discover what rebooting your church might look like for them now?

Consider these coaching questions:

- How can we get clear on what God desires for our church now?
- How can our church be engaged in God's mission in the world?
- What is working in our church now that moves us into God's call?
- What drains our energy/resources without moving us into God's mission for us now?
- What are our best criteria for effective ministry that lives into our mission?
- What programs/experiences consistently fail to meet these criteria?
- What do we need to stop doing so we can focus on priorities to maximize our resources in God's mission for us now?
- What are the three top priorities for the next three years?
- How do we align our resources, staffing, and program organization to accomplish these priorities in three years?
- How do we introduce new directions to our congregation?
- What are the benefits of the proposed focus?
- What are the challenges we will likely face (individually, collectively)?
- What is the best picture for how we will look if taking these priorities seriously?

I'm gradually coming to embrace that the traditional, biblically based five functions of the church have been too formalized and program-based in many traditions. Maybe it's time we preserve and magnify the functions, rather than the forms, of the church in more incarnational, organic language if we want to speak effectively to the twenty-first century. I would propose that functions like relational, redemption, restoration and forgiveness replace the traditional functions many churches embrace–evangelism, discipleship, worship. How do you embrace and express these biblical functions in your ministry design?

How Can We Reboot without Destroying Our Church?

Prayer and spiritual discernment are vital ingredients of a congregational coaching experience. Prayer begins months before the onsite meetings begin and continues throughout the coaching session experiences. The coach's prayer preparation is key in providing the best coaching experience that offers a safe and sacred place and awareness of the Spirit's movement among the people of God. Here is a document given to church leaders as the covenant is established.

Focused Prayer Guide for the Coach Approach to Strategy Planning:
Finding and Embracing Your Church's Future

PURPOSE

1. Provides prayer focus for discernment and relationship building.
2. Provides catalyst for creative and clarifying dialogues between pastor/staff, key leaders, congregation, and community.
3. Provides prayerful forum that helps clarify priorities, gifts, callings, and possibilities for the future.
4. Provides guided times of focused solitude for listening for God's leading, holy nudging.
5. Provides small-and-large-group opportunities to build new relationships and to hear a different generation's perspective on key questions/issues.

PREPARATION—PRIOR TO FIRST ONSITE COACHING SESSION

Challenge and provide focused times for key leaders and congregation to focus on:

1. What does God want us to accomplish in the next four/five months of coaching?
2. Who needs to be involved in the coaching sessions?
3. What do we need to pay attention to during these months?
4. Who would God have me reach out to as a prayer partner during this time (preferably persons outside one's usual friendship circle and age group)?

FOLLOWING COACHING SESSION 1
(WITH PASTOR/STAFF, KEY LEADERS)

Challenge and provide time for key leaders and congregation to engage in focused corporate, individual, and group prayer time (formally and informally).

1. What is working at our church? (Discern through prayer what "working/nonworking" is to mean now.).
2. What is not working at our church?
3. What does God desire for our church in the next two-to-five years?

4. What opportunities are around us that we need to pay attention to as we pray and plan for the future?
5. What partnerships might God be creating to help accomplish His purpose in our community?

FOLLOWING COACHING SESSION 2
(WITH CONGREGATION)

Begin to identify, clarify, and prioritize what we are discerning through prayer.
1. What are we hearing through prayer?
2. What patterns and priorities are emerging in our prayer dialogues?
3. Where is the challenge God is presenting to us as people of faith?
4. What needs to change if we are to follow God's leading?

PREPARATION FOR COACHING SESSION 3
(INTERPRETATION WITH CONGREGATION)

Provide a forum to affirm, celebrate, and give visibility to discovered and embraced plans for the next several years.
1. What are the priorities God desires for us to follow in next few years?
2. What do we need to stop, or reduce resources for, in order to follow our focus?
3. How can we help others see what we see?
4. Who can help us accomplish the discerned goals? What teams are needed?
5. Where are the resources to make these goals become reality?

SUGGESTIONS

- Use key focus/coaching questions in weekly worship bulletins, newsletters, and the church website.
- Encourage small groups, choirs, and families to use questions as sources for prayer, dialogues, Bible studies, and worship focus.
- Regularly invite persons/families/groups to share discovered impressions and learnings with the congregation or their small groups.
- When appropriate, use questions as a framework for worship design, sermons, prayer, and Bible study times.
- Share the questions with all key leadership groups and at the beginning of deacon, council, team, and committee meetings during the coaching time. Provide time for persons to share their impressions, questions, and insights.

Many churches—perhaps most churches—have done things the same way for so long that the way they do church has become part of their belief system. Yet something that may have worked decades ago may no longer work. Some church leaders once found a process rewarding and now are unwilling to suggest deviating from such long-held practices even when they see a need for change. Through congregational coaching, many people will come to the same awareness—that how something is done is not sacred, and embracing change may renew the church.

Consider, for example, church committees. A generation or two ago, serving on a committee gave members a way to contribute. They gave churches a way to get work done and to keep members involved. Today, however, with aging and shrinking attendance, active members in many churches find themselves serving on multiple committees simply to keep the structure alive. They are wed to their polity and can see no other way to keep the work of the church moving forward.

If/when congregations through coaching realize a need for change, what can they do?

One Church's Progress

I had the joy and honor of working with First Baptist Church, Jefferson City, Missouri, in 2011. The old downtown church was facing demographic, economic, and cultural shifts on many fronts. They were seeking ways to face the future with hope, courage, and faith. Doyle Sager, their senior minister, sent me an e-mail while I was working on this book. The hope and significant forward movement he related are so exciting to hear. I asked his permission to share part of that e-mail here as an encouragement to my readers. Hope can be restored to a church—even an old downtown church with an aging congregation—but it takes work, faith, prayer, leadership, and intentionality. Here is what Doyle shared:

UPDATES ON MOVEMENT

1. We have changed business meetings to more of a celebration of ministries, with financial reports coming later in the meeting. Business meeting attendance has dramatically increased.
2. We are engaging even more in our community, city council, transit issues, etc. (This was one aspect that was actually rolling pretty well before you came, but it is getting more focus and intentionality.)

3. Lay leaders are coming up with ministry entrepreneur ideas: since we are so close to the railroad station, we provide winter coats and duffel bags for recently released prisoners, who are often given only a paper sack and have no winter clothes. Amtrak has cooperated beautifully; so has the prison system.

4. All of our 175th anniversary last year was focused on giving ourselves away as an anniversary gift to the community. Lots of events/services/projects were provided. I preached a series this fall (in conjunction with our anniversary), "The Church Has Left the Building," and next April we will dismiss Sunday morning services and do projects around town.

5. We remodeled the narthex from a funeral home atmosphere of, "Shhhh, God is sleeping," to a coffee area with new sofas, tables, and chairs set up bistro style...really pushing the coffee time after services.

6. The biggest change is that we announced in October the transition of our 10:45 service to praise and worship/casual worship (8:15 will remain traditional/blended). We didn't vote on it. Just built a quiet base of support and announced it as the way God is leading, with demographic evidence of whom we are not reaching. We launch this Sunday, January 6. Of course, there was some wailing and gnashing of teeth among some old diehards, but Eddie, the release of positive energy, sense of excitement, and pledges of support were amazing. A new sense of adventure is evident.

Even though we had no budget money to support the equipment and people we needed for worship transition, budget concessions were made to support it. Then out of the blue a very gifted young man who has been trained in praise music in Australia was located by our music pastor and is on board as a volunteer.

As I said, we have a long way to go (and I've been reminding them that worship changes don't matter if we don't practice hospitality).

Stay tuned. God is at work.

Dr. Doyle Sager, Senior Pastor

First Baptist Church

Jefferson City, Missouri

First Baptist Church, Jefferson City, Missouri, like so many others I have worked with, has found movement and hope as they embrace some present realities of church leadership and life. Permit me to capture and quickly summarize some of the discoveries and paths to hope.

Downsizing Committees—a Vital Part of Church Transformation

Many churches have even more committees than they have active members, and they plan to keep it that way. "After all, this is the way we have always done it," is their logic and motivation. The problem is that committees, while they may have worked in past decades, rarely work in today's culture and with today's dual-career marriages and single-parent families. Downsizing or demolishing the committee structure is a vital part of transforming a congregation.

In far too many cases in today's culture, committee structures slow down the decision-making process and often end up as regular or irregular gatherings of people that rarely accomplish anything. Conversation rules, and decisions are avoided to preserve peace or comfort. Other committees are immobilized because of members' protecting or promoting their personal agendas rather than pursuing God's mission through the church. Another reason to downsize committees is that in most situations the committee structure is designed to protect, perpetuate, and resource programs (which is not all bad, but needs to change to being built around mobilizing for mission engagement. Finally, most committees' history is: once you are on a committee, you are on there for life by choice or default. Too often committee membership and participation are limited to active or visible members rather than those churched and unchurched who are passionate about the focus.

Committees tend to create a real or perceived atmosphere that leadership is limited to a few, while most members of the church or community have no voice or avenue for involvement. Such issues, and many others, provide the rationale for rethinking, and reframing the way the work and ministry of the church gets done. In many cases, other processes and options are far more effective in fulfilling the mission of the church and mobilizing the membership to penetrate the community for Christ.

The Biggest Challenge

The biggest challenge in downsizing committees will be the voice of active committee members and established members.

For some, committees are a way of control rather than engagement in mission.

Veteran members will not want to share the load and responsibility because "we know how we want it done and *they* don't."

Others will declare, "The constitution and bylaws and/or the denomination calls for committees, and we must not deviate from those standards."

Still others will say, "Who is going to do all this work if we do not have committees?"

Each of the reasons has some merit, but the true challenge is dealing with the deep emotional nature individuals or groups attach to "their" committee. All rationality and logic give way to the emotional attachments of individuals that often prevent new structures for ministry and decision making to be implemented. This more often than not inhibits the growth of future leaders and prevents the streamlining of decision making, both of which communicate, verbally and nonverbally, to the younger generation and others not currently involved that "we are not wanted here" or "these folks are not really concerned about mission, just maintenance and tradition."

Another dimension of this big challenge is that many churches hold on tenaciously to a deep value and longstanding tradition that "we need all these committees." "Pastor Bob or Deacon Sam or Elder Joe or Jane started this committee, and we must keep it alive!" Such deep emotional attachment and value will present the greatest obstacle to moving forward to new structures for mobilizing ministry. To make these shifts well, you must explore or change this value before you change the structures. Another option might include asking this question: "How can you live more effectively and efficiently into the values you hold?" Or, "How might you express these values/traditions in more effective and efficient ways?" (See my book *Making Shifts without Making Waves* for more help.)

Fresh Methods for Getting the Work of the Church Accomplished

Here are some methods for mobilizing to consider, and something of the rationale behind the suggestion to shift away from committees to new methods.

Short-term task force groups are great for tasks that may be seasonal (holidays, Eucharist or Lord's Supper, baptisms). These have some predictability but could easily be short-term to accomplish a task. Then the group is done unless they have some evaluation tips they want to pass along to the next group for the next season of activity.

Invitation teams provide an intentional entry point for persons who need an invitation to join a team or group for a short-term project or ministry task. Volunteers are great, but not everyone is aware enough or extroverted enough to volunteer. To feel like they are valued and belong to the community of faith, many people need to be invited, asked to be a part of something. People on this team are highly observant of those around them. They always listen for a person's passion, calling, or interest, and how/where that might strengthen a choir, ensemble, mission team, a short-term task force group, or a focused team. These invitation team members are warm and inviting in their approach and are keenly aware of the host of ministry options in and through the church. Their role is "on the spot" (not taking it to or through a committee) to engage the person(s) in conversation: "Have you ever thought about...?" "I think you would be great at...!" "Would you like me to introduce you to some folks who can tell you more about...?"

Ongoing foundational committees can handle the few ongoing functions of the church. They can be elected annually and rotate to preserve some continuity of information, but not control. Functions such as trustees, elders, deacons, personnel, finance, stewardship/generosity continue to work well for a committee structure. Most everything else can be outside of committee structures.

Short-term focused teams are great for streamlining decision making, mobilizing people of passion, and integrating churched, unchurched, dechurched, and rechurched people who share common interests. The short-term focus is far more attractive to persons in dual-career marriages, single parents, or adults outside the system who are curious and would like an easy place to experiment without a deep level of commitment initially. Focused teams offer this option. Most short-term focused teams serve for four-to-six, maybe ten weeks at most. They plan, conduct, and evaluate a project or mission experience; or engage in community missions, vacation Bible studies, flowers for church events, hospitality for focused groups (new members, guests), Bible study planning for adults, worship planning for a seasonal emphasis, children or youth events, outreach focused on target groups/places, etc.

Engaged faith communities can allow clusters of passionate, called, and gifted lay and/or clergy persons to become family as they work on common mission adventures, face new learning curves in faith and skill, and care for one another and those they serve. Their gifts of pastoring, leadership, mercy, administration, teaching, etc., bring them together to be and do church in places of opportunity, openness, and challenge. They pray, worship, and work together in intentional ways to make a difference in one another's lives, but also in the lives of those they feel called to serve in the midst of—as the presence of Christ.

Because of their short-term service in groups or teams, these faith communities often find persons of passion who want more, or to go deeper. These faith communities practice loving accountability to help one another excel in their calling and gifting, and to retain their focus and intentionality in ministry. These communities might be a cluster of families, friends, men's or women's groups, Bible study groups, or task forces that feel called to go to the next level in their spiritual formation and engagement. The community decides the time, commitment level, and focus of their community. These teams are accountable to the congregation for regular reports, invitations to participate short-term, and to engage themselves and the larger congregation in focused prayer on behalf of the faith community.

This system of mobilization is implemented through staff, elders, and/or a leadership team that coordinates, plans, schedules, and alerts an invitation team of opportunities. Everyone involved in short- or long-term ministry ventures must be included on a complete ministry roster list and in commissioning services for all who serve in long-term committee assignments or short-term teams or task force groups. Then periodically those who serve share their perceptions of what, where, and how God is working in and through the church. This can be done in quarterly church family gatherings or weekly as ministry updates in newsletters, web pages, worship, and/or small-group gatherings. Affirmation, encouragement, commissioning, and reporting build in accountability, the power of focus that creates and sustains missional momentum in the life of the church and shows the depth and distribution of leadership—critical elements of moving a congregation forward!

Discouragement comes easily to plateaued or declining churches who can't seem to make any forward progress to engage God's mission. The good news is that many churches are moving from stagnation to transformation.

Jen Hatmaker, in *7: An Experimental Mutiny against Excess*, wrote this incredible description of what God is up to these days:

> Something marvelous and powerful is happening in the church. The Bride is awakening and the Spirit is rushing. It is everywhere.

This movement is not contained within a denomination or demographic, not limited to a region or country. It's sweeping up mothers and pastors and teenagers and whole congregations. A stream became a current, and it is turning into a raging flood. It is daily gathering conspirators and defectors from the American Dream. It is cresting with the language of the gospel: the weak made strong, the poor made rich, the proud made humble.

The body of Christ is mobilizing in unprecedented numbers. Jesus is staging a massive movement to bind up the brokenhearted and proclaim freedom for captives. The trumpet is blowing. We are on the cusp, on the side of the Hero. So while we're mistakenly warring with ourselves, Jesus is waging war on injustice and calling us to join Him.[1]

Church leaders and faith communities face very real challenges, desiring to keep the existing generation of members (from the church culture era) while reaching a new generation of members (from an entirely different and more secular culture). Such challenges are often overwhelming and, more often than not, neither the lay or clergy leaders are properly equipped for the demanding challenges.

Returning to health calls for a plan, a desire, and a willingness to follow the plan into greater health for a more fruitful and fulfilling future. Consider the following as a guide and way of self-assessment.

Preparing Today's Church for Tomorrow

CONCEPTS NOT TO BE IGNORED

- Prayerfully consider the focus for your future.
- Be proactive rather than reactive in praying, planning, and organizing for ministry and mission.
- Be strategic, realizing you can't be all things to all people.
- Be intentional about balancing maintenance and mission when budgeting, staffing, calendaring, programming, etc.
- Prepare for a multicultural, multiethnic, multigenerational population.
- Engage change/transition management skill sets among leaders.
- Consider prayerfully the church's response to the rapid change in culture, technology, and pace of life.
- Consider decentralizing your ministry rather than building bigger buildings.

SOME PRACTICAL RESPONSES TO CONSIDER

- Learn to create sacred space and place for all age groups.
- Streamline decision making while practicing collaborative leadership that focuses on achieving consensus rather than casting votes.
- Balance programming, staffing, and budgeting around come and go structures.
- Build "white space/sacred space" into your church calendar and protect it.
- Consider multi-career, part-time, mission-focused staffing.
- Use boomer retirees and expertise.
- Learn to build missional-based partnerships among churches and communities.
- Learn to create win-win scenarios among different generations.
- Invest in and require continuing education for all staff and key lay leaders—at least one event each year and a planned sabbatical.
- Focus more on missional engagement than membership management.
- Create mentoring/apprenticeships for next-generation leaders built on discipleship principles.
- Create fresh expressions/traditions and rituals that honor God, Scripture, and core values of the congregation.
- Consider what alignments/partnerships serve your church's vision and values best and focus financial and leadership investment on these partnerships.
- Rethink family ministry in light of the new family structures emerging in our culture.
- Outsource as much as possible to minimize staff and facility expenses while ensuring excellence in programming/ministry.

Much of my passion and focus in ministry is to work with leaders, churches, and denominations to discover transforming solutions that transform their faith community into who God is calling them to be. My approach is mostly the coach approach that focuses on discovery and discernment more than declarations or prescriptions. I can certainly offer my expertise in a subject area if desired. See the flyer on the next page I share with those seeking to reboot their Christian education ministry.

Are You Seeking Solutions for:

- Being an overprogrammed church?
- Declining participation and interest in Bible study?
- Little evidence of transformation in members' lives?
- Diminishing leader morale and effectiveness?
- Dealing with time-poor families?
- Reaching and assimilating new members?
- Connecting worship to Bible study and missional engagement?
- Maximizing your limited resources?

Consider...

Rebooting Your Christian Education Ministry
- Discern God's vision for your church's future.
- Improve leader morale and engagement.
- Bring freshness to your programming.
- Align programming with ministry vision.
- Engage in a collaborative approach to deepen
- impact and broaden leadership base.
- Streamline programming.

Eddie Hammett, a certified professional church and clergy coach, provides a coach approach designed to engage leaders and congregation in rebooting, rethinking, retooling, and refreshing the Christian education ministry in your local church in ways that engage leaders to deepen the impact and influence of your ministry in the day-to-day world.

COACHING & CONSULTING SERVICES PROVIDED BY EDDIE HAMMETT

Eddie is a seasoned church and denominational leader who has served churches and individuals for more than thirty years. He is president of Transforming Solutions, LLC, and author of seven books, including his best-sellers *Reaching People under 40 While Keeping People over 60* and *Making Shifts without Making Waves*. Eddie is committed to improving the effectiveness of ministry of the local church in a rapidly changing world. His insights are practical, his coaching is transformational, and his commitment to Christ and the church are unmistakable. His presence will stretch you, inspire you, and encourage you along the journey. Visit his website www.TransformingSolutions.org or e-mail him for additional information at Eddie@transformingsolutions.org

What will be the likely consequences if you do not reboot your church now?

COACHING QUESTIONS

1. What speaks to your situation in the promotion above?
2. What is missing?
3. How might you share this information with others?
4. What will be the benefits of engaging in this experience now?

Creating a Strategy That Works

Making any shifts in how we do church often calls for a time of discernment, prayer, reflection, and self-assessment, plus consistent times for collective thinking on the part of leaders and congregation. A critical piece of any coaching relationship is co-creating a coaching covenant/agreement that guides the relationship from beginning to end. Many coaching relationships drift and lose momentum because the covenant is not in place or is not used effectively.

This is my framework for beginning a coaching covenant conversation. I like it to be simple, focused, clear, and collaborative. Some coaches are much more detailed and use more paperwork. I like the simple approach. I often take significant time in conversation with the person or group that is engaging my services to be sure we are clear upfront about our covenant.

Co-creating a Congregational Coaching Covenant

The sample covenant on page 140 is a useful tool to explain what congregational coaching is and to set or clarify everyone's expectations at the beginning of the coaching relationship.

Covenant for Congregational Coaching
(Framework for Focus, Accountability, and Forward Movement)

- Coaching is about the church's discernment and decisions, not the coach's prescription.
- Coaching is about forward movement, not untangling conflict of past issues.
- Coaching assumes a significant degree of health of leaders and congregation.
- Congregational coaching is rooted in prayer, spiritual discernment, and the openness of a congregation to follow God's leading.
- Congregational coaching brings no judgment or preference to the coaching relationship in order to provide a safe place to explore and dialogue.
- Coaching is about stretching beyond your comfort zones and pushing through fears and anxieties to follow the best discernment of God's direction.
- Coaching is about intentionality, prioritization, and collaborative learning designed to invite as many voices as possible into the process.
- Coaching is about deepening a congregation's learning and moving dialogue into meaningful actions that will move the congregation forward.
- Congregational coaching calls on key leaders, pastor, staff to be prayerful and intentional in facilitating prayer and follow up on plans before, between, and after coaching sessions.
- Congregational coaching is a peer-learning, collaborative process. To sustain focus and momentum gained, a congregation may benefit from annual check-ups or periodic cluster gatherings with other like congregations on a similar journey.
- The actions taken are the decision of the congregation and not that of the coach.
- Congregational coaching calls for an intentional commitment to pray, reflect, and dialogue in order to discern focus, priority, and forward movement.

WHAT NEEDS TO BE NEGOTIATED?

1. Desired outcomes for the process:_____
   _____
   _____
2. Frequency and number of needed coaching sessions/time/target groups: _____
3. Desired role/function of coach: _____
4. Costs involved: _____

19

The Power of Focus, Prioritization, and Mobilization

"HOPE IS A DAY THE END OF WHICH WE MAY NEVER SEE."
—Edward Counsel, *Maxims*

Lying in a hospital bed for months on end, I had plenty of time to ask why? Why had this happened to me? Why now? Why hadn't I seen the warning signs and responded more quickly to get help? Why was it taking me so long to get better?

Churches, caught in decline or on a plateau, also ask why? We started this book in the preface by looking at some of the *why* questions churches are asking. Let's look at them again.

- Why has our church plateaued?
- Why are so few young leaders going into church-based ministries?
- Why are so few interested in church these days?
- Why are so many churches going out of business and having to close their doors?
- Why are the number of unchurched increasing and the number of churched decreasing?
- Why are our churches downsizing while community spiritual needs and appetites are increasing?

Your church may have asked these same questions or similar why questions. You may never know all the answers to why, but you can be instrumental in turning your church around so that it has a

viable, thriving, promising future. Through the power of focus, prioritization, and mobilization, your church can turn *why* questions
into *why not!?* Part of the answer may be moving beyond missional
to incarnational.

As North America becomes less churched and more spiritually
thirsty, we are called to deepen our investment in people to earn the
right to be heard, to be introduced to others, and to be welcomed
by the unchurched without becoming part of the unchurched. John
14:6 indicates Christ came and "dwelt among us"–He moved in
and shared life with us–the very essence of incarnational ministry.
Jesus calls *us* to be *in* the world but not *of* the world. Churches
today face the same challenge God faced before He sent His Son
into the world. God had tried through prophets, kings, and wars
to get his message across, but to no avail. Then He sent His Son
that we might know. So, how might the incarnational experience
and commitment differ from missional experiences? Incarnational
experiences are captured and find focus and momentum in the
incubators of:

- **INviting**–This is about believers being invited by nonchurched or nonbelievers into their world as friends, fellow
travelers, guides, and spiritual friends. This is not for a "bait
and switch" role reversal, but genuinely being friends with
no strings attached.
- **INtroducing**–This has more to do with experiences in
which the believer and nonbeliever,, or nonchurched
person, are willing and intentional about introducing and
being introduced to each other's friendship circles. Again,
for no reason other than being a friend, colleague, fellow
journeyman–whatever roles seem to be mutually agreeable
at this time.
- **INclusion**–This represents an even deeper, more relational, more intentional time of seeking places and experiences
where such inclusion is mutually desired, enjoyed, and
accepted.
- **INtimacy**–This step deepens the relationship even more.
This has more to do with sharing of heart and feelings about
life issues, celebrations, and struggles. It might involve attending weddings, christening children, being present at
funerals for the deaths of family members, etc.
- **INvesting**–This takes the relationship to another level of
being purposeful of investing in each other's spiritual journey; pursuit of life questions; seeking out how, where, and

who God is; and where we connect with Him in life's meanings and purposes.

- **INvolved**–This step is a formal, mutual decision that this relationship is beneficial to both parties on their spiritual journeys. They share what they are discovering, learning, and experiencing as they learn about each other's faith life, church journey, and where they sense the next steps to be for their journey through life together.

Note of explanation: The funnel diagram on page 44 is simply to indicate that work of incarnation often begins in a vast and often whirling and uncertain space and gradually moves, by the Spirit's leading and the obedience of persons involved, to a focus where insights and convictions emerge that make the power of God known in a person's life and space.

MISSIONAL FOCUS	INCARNATIONAL FOCUS
Outward focused	Acceptance/Invitation focused
How do we engage people outside the walls of the church?	How do we earn acceptance and invitation into churched/unchurched relationships?
Message of influence and impact	Relational messages of reconciliation, redemption, hope, healing, and health
About being out among the unchurched serving people through relief efforts through partnerships	About being in with, not insulated from, persons unlike you ("In the world, not of the world")
Often ask, "What can we do?"	Often ask, "Who do we need to be?"
Often ask, "How can we serve?"	Often ask, "How can we be salt, light, and leaven in this situation now?"
Committed to an assigned task of serving	Committed to walking with and living among in a way to please Christ

For churches to set new priorities, they will need a new worldview and churchview, a new sense of how to do and be church, a new commitment to joining God's mission for that particular congregation. Particularly for churches grieving about their past numbers in nickels and noses, understanding a new kind of growth is essential. Few churches have examined their culture to consider what it communicates. Those inside have often been there so long they have no idea that they even have a distinct culture, much less one that intentionally communicates to newcomers. A coach can help them become aware of just what their culture is and what it communicates.

Deepening how we live *into* the world and as the church in the world today calls for a new metric, a new way of measuring impact and influence to determine our effectiveness in being salt, light, and leaven in the world as the body of Christ. Maybe we need to be evaluating/tracking engagement rather than just attendance or participation in programming. Consider...

Moving from Missional to Incarnational Ministry Engagement

The essence and challenge of incarnational ministry is found in *showing up*, being *intentionally engaged* in relationships that *manifest gifts and fruit of the Spirit* that *deepen impact, influence, and fruit bearing* in *keeping with the character and presence of Christ.* Below are some examples for review and illustration to move you or your church forward in incarnational ministries. Evaluate where you are now in each of the incarnational indicators from 1 (minimal attention given to this area) to 10 (maximum attention given). LETS talk about this

COACHING QUESTIONS

1. How would you rate your congregation's incarnational engagement?
2. What would the stretch (moving beyond your comfort zone) look like for you? your church?
3. Which one area will you focus on in the next six months? What will this look like?
4. How will you know when you are effectively living into the call and presence of Christ in these relationships?

INCARNATIONAL INDICATORS TO CONSIDER	INCARNATIONAL MANIFESTATION POSSIBILITIES	SELF-ASSESSMENT/ GOAL SETTING
INviting—Engagement that yields opportunity to invite or be invited to a deeper, more trusting relationship	Coffee shop dialogues Recreational experiences	1 (minimal) to 10 (maximum)
INtroducing— Engagement that yields others' introducing believer friends to nonbeliever or nonchurched friends	Introduced into relationships with friends of one or both persons involved	1 (minimal) to 10 (maximum)
INclusion— Engagement that creates atmosphere of being included in circles of relationship outside church connections	Sharing focused, intentional time at coffee shop or mealtime/ recreational dialogues	1 (minimal) to 10 (maximum)
INtimacy—Engagement that yields trusting, open conversations without judgment by anyone	Engaging in dialogues and experiences that offer emotional, spiritual, prayerful support over issues of struggle, pain, confusion—probably on turf where participants are most comfortable	1 (minimal) to 10 (maximum)
INvesting— Engagement that is a mutual opportunity for investing in each other's life as trusted friends	Investing time, energy, resources in building trust and moving forward in health, hope, healing, and trust building	1 (minimal) to 10 (maximum)
INvolved—A deepening of engagement and involvement that is forward moving toward deeper health, hope, and maturity that is mutually respected and practiced	Purposeful, mutually meaningful relationship that is built on mutual respect, honesty, and a desire to move forward in faith life	1 (minimal) to 10 (maximum)

20

Making Events More Meaningful Experiences of Transformation

A COACH APPROACH TO IMPROVING MEETINGS

"WISDOM COMES WITH THE ABILITY TO BE STILL.
JUST LOOK AND JUST LISTEN. NO MORE IS NEEDED.
BEING STILL, LOOKING, AND LISTENING ACTIVATES THE
NON-CONCEPTUAL INTELLIGENCE WITHIN YOU.
LET STILLNESS DIRECT YOUR WORDS AND ACTIONS."
—Eckhart Tolle, *Stillness Speaks*

The process of recovery involves many appointments, visits to a variety of doctors and therapists, engaging in wise shopping for heart-healthy foods, exercise routines, journaling, engaging with my coach to help needed alignment and change happen,…and the list goes on. Many events and experiences called me to deeper understanding of finding meaning in all the meetings and appointments I faced in daily life. I could fight them, simply walk through them like a robot, or learn to find deeper meaning and significance in them. This called forth a mindset and value shift in my previous routines.

Most churches, judicatories, businesses, and even groups of various types plan meetings as part of their functions. Often the primary function of some groups and employees seems to be to plan and attend meetings. While meetings have their place in coordination, collaboration, and carrying out a group's mission, many meetings seem meaningless and fruitless. Meetings can move a group forward in function and mission, or meetings can kill or distract from a group's function and mission. Patrick Lencioni has given us a great book, *Death by Meeting*, that brings clarity to fatal and fruitful meetings.[1] What would make meetings more effective? How do you make events you plan more meaningful and fruitful experiences that move the organization forward in function and effectiveness?

One way to improve effectiveness and meaning is to use the coach approach in planning and conducting the meeting. The coach approach has more to do with deepening and broadening leadership and ownership of ideas and projects than just talking about the project or ideas. The coach approach creates collaboration and generates ownership and excitement along with anticipation of, "What's next?" and, "What will make this better?" Coaching is about forward movement, asking powerful questions, and working from the agenda of the person(s) being coached (PBC). (See *Christian Coaching for Leaders* by Chad Hall and Linda Miller, and *The Complete Idiot's Guide to Coaching for Excellence* by Jane Creswell, for more of the basics of coaching.[2]) Take some time to evaluate the meetings you are a part of.

- How effective are the meetings you plan or attend?
- What makes meetings so meaningless and unproductive at times?

Another Way of Crafting Meetings

All too often, a schedule of meetings births another schedule of meetings. Sometimes annual planning consists of what we did last year and the dates for the same events next year. Planning events is critical in moving organizations forward, however. Because events are so frequent, they often lose intentionality, focus, and even meaning when it comes to accomplishing a declared mission of the organization that creates or sustains forward movement. *Another way of crafting such a gathering is to begin with the mission statement, the elements of focus, and goals for the organization during a given period of time and using these as lenses that serve as framework for designing an experience, not just a meeting.*

What if you planned experiences rather than events?

As an illustration, in the Cooperative Baptist Fellowship of North Carolina, where I serve as church and clergy coach, it is clear from our name, mission, and focus that we are about:

- Cooperation
- Fellowship
- Collaboration
- Missional ministry and living

Many of the events we plan for our members and partners keep these objectives in mind but occasionally lose focus in the frequency and sequencing of the events. Our mission and focus might be strengthened more if we started with the ingredients of the experiences we are seeking to model and create. The coach in me wonders, *What if we planned an annual calendar (in CBFNC and our related councils, partners, and churches) around experiences rather than events?* Making events more meaningful experiences hinges on a powerful question: How can these core values/elements of focus be manifested in…(the experience being planned)?

Consider some *key experiences* to be achieved and some coaching questions that may help make an event for a CBFNC group or church a more fruitful, focused, intentional experience that moves us one step forward in our agreed-upon mission.

COOPERATION

- What are the elements of effective cooperation?
- How will we know when cooperation is achieved?
- How will cooperation manifest itself in…?
- How will we manifest more cooperation now?

FELLOWSHIP

- What makes up fellowship?
- How do we measure and experience fellowship?
- What happens when fellowship is not present in (event/meeting)?
- What shifts are needed now to make our fellowship more effective?

COLLABORATION

- How and where do we experience collaboration best?
- What are the benefits of collaboration?
- What are the challenges of collaboration?
- Where and how can we be more collaborative now?

MISSIONAL

- What is the best example of missional we know?
- What and how can we learn from this?
- How does missional living impact and influence?
- How will this meeting make us more missional now?

Applying principles to your context involves three objectives. Leaders (and often participants) need to find answers to:

1. What are the core values/foci of our group's mission?
2. How can these values be integrated as building blocks for the experience we are planning now?
3. How will we evaluate the result?

This chart might be a useful guide as you create more meaningful experiences.

Making Events More Meaningful Experiences
(Moving the Mission Forward through Events)
Example based on CBFNC Foci

CORE VALUES/FOCI OF ORGANIZATION	POSSIBLE EXPRESSIONS OF CORE VALUES	HOW TO INTEGRATE INTO EXPERIENCE	DESIRED OUTCOMES
Cooperation	Working together; complimenting rather than competing	Clarify ground rules; Challenge to and seek to be complimentary	Agreement, common direction, partnering in shared missions
Fellowship	Create open and inclusive atmosphere; learn about various personal preferences and traditions	Invite persons to share about themselves and two distinctives about themselves or family	Educate about distinctives/preferences; see and value diversity as a gift and put it to work in the group
Collaboration	Incorporate others in planning, conducting, and evaluating Consider ways different people groups can work together	Build task forces around diversity of ideas and people groups; celebrate new ideas and opportunities	Build and celebrate new relationships and ideas; share new discoveries of how the body works together
Missional	Equally divide budget and planning for inside and beyond existing members	Engage and evaluate effectiveness of inside and beyond experiences	Gain factual understanding of behavior rather than just subjective perception
Incarnational	"Move in" to new relationships and being invited into other's relationships	Become intentional in relationship building and follow through	Build mutual trust and respect

Time to Evaluate

Are we still planning meetings and events? Yes, to some degree, but the meeting is less important than the core value experiences we are seeking to move forward during and after the event. Every element of the event can fuel and create forward movement for the mission of the organization. Once these core values are clear, the designing of the experiences is filled with more intentionality, energy, and meaning.

Here's a final coaching tip most leaders will like, but many will struggle to embrace: establish a clear time frame for the event, experience, or meeting. Without firm beginning and ending times, often frustration emerges; some feel their personal schedules are not being valued; and far too often we keep talking just because no ending time is agreed upon. Try it and see what happens. Then share your experiences with me at EHammett@cbfnc.org.

Deepening the impact of our corporate experiences is critical, especially in worship. "How do we remain one church when we have multiple worship services?" is a question many churches and members wrestle with in the age of multiple worship services. Consider these possibilities and their probable impact. What areas do you resonate with?

"Assimilation and building of the church fellowship *does not just happen. It must be intentionally and prayerfully nurtured and planned for* in the diversity of twenty-first–century churches. Multiple services, while frequently positioning churches for numerical growth, create many challenges but also many opportunities for each age group to have experiences that are meaningful to them and for connecting with God, their peers, and other age groups as well."

Another challenge in improving the effectiveness of a church experience has to do with balancing structures to prevent duplication or competition for people or for energy.. Consider auditing your church functions.

Church Function Audit

DIRECTIONS

Take an opportunity to self-assess the current and potential church functions. Make a list of all arenas of your church programming/ministries and indicate your opinion of their *primary* function.

Creating Community among Multiple Worship Services
(For Deepening of Fellowship and Meaning for All Ages)

COMMUNITY-BUILDING POSSIBILITIES	MEASURING IMPACT
Share leadership—faith stories, music, drama, readings, litanies, prayer...	Presence, integration of all age groups and gifts in worship
Close the information gap between services and people groups	Integrated worship folder, announcements, media; use pictures and bios of new members; have designated Facebook pages, websites with common links
Share stories celebrating God's work in and through attendees in each service	Video, audio, downloadable recordings; share recordings in each worship setting to inform, Inspire, and celebrate God's work among the people
Family introductions—intentional mentoring or supportive relationships	Create database of ministry connections to facilitate mentoring, discipleship, pastoral care, and assimilation into mission and ministry inside and beyond the church walls
Visit each other's services, Bible study classes, and groups to nurture relationships and introduce people	Intentional introductions, networking, sharing of stories; plan intergenerational learning experiences and fellowship gatherings; What can you/are you learning from each other's journey in faith and life?
Create and nurture prayer partnerships between generations and worship services; share discoveries, experiences in services, and classes/groups.	Sharing, recording, and hearing the movement of God through prayer and nurturing of relationships; create a page on websites or hallway bulletin boards to share connections and powerful learnings
Intentional, prayerful church buddy connections—personal, career, recreational, family-type variations	Maintain database of persons seeking connections in each category, a "craigslist" for church and community connections
Holiday hosts—invite persons into one's home or holiday gatherings	Focus might include singles, students, or others away from home during holidays; homeless; those seeking employment; or persons with health-care issues.

DEFINITION OF CATEGORIES

Come Structures–Inviting people to "come to" the church for gatherings.

Go Structures–Creating opportunities for people "to go" out of the building into places or people groups as the church.

Open Groups–Groups that are intentional about being open to guests, nonmembers; people can come at their leisure.

Closed Groups–Groups intentionally closed in order to build fellowship, trust, or work on deepening discipleship.

Inward Focused–Efforts, energies, and resources are focused inward to cultivate and perpetuate class/group fellowship and mission.

Outward Focused–Efforts, energies, and resources are focused outward in order to reach the needs of others.

PROGRAM/ MINISTRY	COME STRUC- TURE	GO STRUC- TURE	OPEN GROUP	CLOSED GROUP	IN- WARD FOCUSED	OUT- WARD FOCUSED
Ex. SS Class	X			X	X	
Ex. Choir						

COACHING QUESTIONS

1. Review your entries. What does this say about your church?
2. What would make it better?
3. How does this chart reinforce/complement your church's vision/mission?
4. What are the consequences if nothing changes?

In doing church audits over the years, I consistently encounter five signs of hope in church functions that seem to move the congregation deeper in faith and greater effectiveness in biblical functions.

Five Signs of Hope for a Church

Here are five signs of hope I've noted in churches that are moving forward in today's world:

1. Openness to the Spirit
2. Obedience to the Spirit's leading

3. Courageous leaders and congregations open to taking risks in connecting with the hurts in the world
4. Openness to collaboration, partnership, and alliances with persons and groups sharing common vision/calling
5. Discovered and embraced focus that allows them (as leaders and churches) to say no to much and yes to their unique calling

A final challenge some church audits reveal has to do with the effectiveness and value of the midweek services. Consider these possibilities.

Putting Meaning into Midweek Services
(Exploring Options for Wednesday Night Church)

POPULAR, BUT OFTEN ROUTINE AND UNFRUITFUL FOR MOVING CHURCH FORWARD IN FAITH OR FUNCTION

1. *Evening fellowship meal*–Often sitting with same friends and family rather than broadening friendship base or intergenerational relationships.
2. *Prayer and Bible study*–Often pastor leads a small group of senior adults who expect the pastor to teach them. It often becomes another Sunday school class or mini-worship service rather than a serious study or prayer time.
3. *Age-related study groups*–Often topical studies that are more for age-group fellowship than transformation or deepening of relationships.

"What happened to Wednesday night commitment from our members?"
"How can we get the young people to come on Wednesday nights?"
"If we only had the same crowd on Wednesday we used to have, our church would grow again!"

WHAT WILL BREATHE NEW LIFE INTO MIDWEEK SERVICES? ("CAN THESE DRY BONES LIVE AGAIN?")
Consider other options and their possible impact on you and your church.

1. Commit to building intergenerational relationships with new friends through fellowship meal and appropriate studies or mentoring relationships (Possible topics/mentoring relationships might include: career mentors, caring of aging parents, coping with the empty or refilled nest, etc.)

2. Be intentional about building database and network of persons who have recovered from:
    a. being downsized at work.
    b. heart surgery, cancer, or other medical issues.
    c. dysfunctional families or behaviors.
    d. other.
3. Flip Sunday school time to Wednesday evenings and only have worship/praise on Sundays. Advantages include:
    a. Frees up Sunday morning for family time at home.
    b. Provides more space, time, and energy for building relationships before, during, and after worship.
    c. Provides for more substantive age-group or intergenerational-focused Bible study on Wednesday evening that can evolve from mealtime to classwork.
4. Create "J terms" for Wednesday evenings that are quarterly, short-term, targeted groupings for missional or functional purposes:
    a. Four-to-six-week groupings with clearly defined outcomes.
    b. Leadership development for existing and future leaders.
    c. Groups for nurturing meaningful intergenerational connections.
    d. Between each four-to-six-week grouping, create and bless "Sabbath space" for family time, outreach, inreach, missional activity, rest, and reflection (four-to-six-week Sabbaths with no committee meetings, etc.).
5. Music/mission focus for all age groups.
6. Create a leadership academy for all community and church leaders. Offer excellent training, networking, partnership-building opportunities as a gift to the community.
7. "Zoe" Groups—Use the coach approach to connect life experiences, biblical truths, and forward movement in faith and function.
8. Consider changing Wednesday services to another day/ time.
9. Offer midweek Bible study and lunch for seniors on Wednesday noon rather than in the evening. Other age groups do midweek Bible study/prayer at home, in community groups, or at work.
10. Create and nurture mentoring relationships for young families, business leaders, entrepreneurs as part of building discipling mentoring relationships.

21

How Churches Can Be Community without Becoming Cliques

"OF ALL THE FORMS OF WISDOM,
HINDSIGHT IS BY GENERAL CONSENT THE LEAST MERCIFUL,
THE MOST UNFORGIVING."
—John Fletcher, in Jean-Claude Favez's *Holocaust*

One of my most frustrating experiences during my health crisis was to get my caregivers, doctors, nurses, and physical therapists to talk with one another. I had to realize this was not just about me. My recovery was dependent on all of us talking together, comparing notes, and working toward the same or at least similar goals. Once we learned this lesson, it was far less frustrating for all of us, and recovery became much more fulfilling. Building a community of recovery was far more helpful than approaching recovery as a solo experience.

I had a stretching and engaging conversation recently with fifteen new residents who seemed unchurched, dechurched, or were struggling rechurched persons (seeking to replant themselves in a new church) in my community. It was not a planned conversation, but rather one of those divine appointments coming forth from an intentional prayer life and learning to pay attention to what God brings in front of me and having the courage to step into it!

I simply asked a question, "What are you looking for in the community that you have not yet found?" It was like the question opened the floodgates for their bottled-up responses that were just waiting for a listening ear! Some of their responses included:

"Where's the best place to...(looking for best stores, services, schools, social events)?"

"Where can we get connected to music in the area? We're musicians and lovers of music and want to get connected!"

"Who are the best doctors in town?"

Then the clincher for me came when someone said, "We've visited some churches in the area looking for community, but all we experienced were cliques!" I could not resist getting them to clarify their experiences, and they were very willing. In fact, the group jumped into the conversation! It was stimulating and an obvious need for many. Now I'm working to learn from the conversation: How can churches be community without becoming cliques?

Church people want community; in fact, we treasure our church family, our class members, and declare openly, "We are the friendliest church in town!" We put out signs: "Everyone welcome!" Great public relations for those inside, but it is so often diametrically opposed to the experience of many who visit!

A retired pastor's wife recently made this statement on my Facebook page in response to this chapter title. "I taught assimilation and hospitality in our churches for decades, and now as a member I see and experience things differently. We are often ignored, isolated to sit or eat by ourselves during family night meals and other church gatherings. No one invites us to sit with them or to meet them or their family and friends. Even when we reach out first, we feel like outsiders, intruders, and like we are disturbing their family environment. How sad for us, and I fear to think how totally unchurched persons might feel or respond."

Most church people do not intend to make outsiders feel this way, but it does happen far more frequently than most church folks want to acknowledge. Church members often fail to consider that some behaviors build barriers. These include:

1. When we pray for our friends by name amid outsiders in a gathering, they feel even more unwanted and like you do not want them to know about your friends.
2. Failing to introduce yourself and your friends and family members by name communicates an isolating atmosphere for outsiders.
3. Failing to take the first step and initiative to greet persons you do not recognize causes persons to feel unwanted.
4. Unwillingness to wear name tags and give guests an invitation and personal escort to your class, their children's

classes, or to other church events is seen as "we're not wanted here."

5. Not having clear signage in strategic locations and in language and clarity outsiders can understand is a barrier. (You might even invite outsiders/guests to help you design and place the signs that speak to them.)

Enough of the barrier builders, how can churches create community without becoming cliques? Here are some thoughts to consider:

1. Take note of each of the previous statements and refocus sensitivity and behaviors.
2. Always have space available for guests/newcomers on every pew, in every classroom, and and at fellowship table gatherings. Communicate verbally and relationally, "We would love to have you (and your friend or family) join us." Always be willing to make room for guests and even give up your chair/pew for others! Research tells us that every newcomer needs to know at least six people by name and affiliations within six weeks or that person is not likely to stay in the church or gathering.
3. Take initiative and greet anyone you do not know by name. Introduce yourself and acknowledge, "I'm working to learn new people in our church. I don't know your name. I'm _____. I'm sorry if you are a longtime member here, and I'm just now learning your name, but I'm trying now to do better."
4. Create opportunity to follow up with guests by exchanging phone numbers, job/career information, and/or e-mail addresses. Ask, "What can I do to help you or your family/ friends learn about our church? I'll be glad to get in touch and help you find answers to your questions. We want you to feel welcome as we become family."
5. Create a hospitality or membership inquirer team designated to create, plan, host, and evaluate regular experiences for inquirers and newcomers. This can take many forms, but must be deliberate, casual, and in a comfortable setting. Some suggestions include:
   - *Pastor/staff gathering with all guests/inquirers in pastor/staff homes,* maybe on a Sunday night while deacons lead regular evening service at church. This creates a warm, small-group atmosphere where pastoral visits with all can be done quickly, communication can be created among all newcomers/guests, and the presence of a few

carefully selected church members can begin a friendship that nurtures everyone and gives them "church
buddies."

- *Banquet for newcomers and guests* held at the church. Plan
a special time with a few well-selected church members
to host each dining table–a time for greetings and sharing of church history stories that are personal, then taking them on a guided tour of facilities led by members
sharing personal stories as they walk through history
and facilities; then return for question-and-answer time
with pastor/staff/deacons. Before leaving the banquet,
everyone knows everyone at their tables or at the event
by name, family membership, careers, school, children/
schools, and any affinity group that seems nurturing for
deepening friendships. Share contact information and
create a church buddy system for each family present.
- *A social media page* for all newcomers/guests for community building online: an avenue for communication, questions, and answers. This works great for those who prefer
social media as their major communication avenue.
- *Photos of newcomers* in church newsletters, guests registry,
and/or church bulletin boards.
- *A new member/inquirers classroom experience* or a retreat
with this group to deepen relationships and provide a
forum for clarifying more of the mission and focus of
the church. This should be no more than a three-to five-
hour experience.
- *Membership presentation.* Present the class of newcomers
to the congregation as a group of new members once
a quarter. This offers encouragement and diffuses for
some the element of fear of being up front by oneself,
and it helps create community among newcomers.
- *Regular seasonal reunions* of all newcomers/new members, introducing them to another group of established
members in a small-group, casual setting. Then invite
all to share with a larger group what they learned about
and from one another.
- *The new member team/hospitality team calls all "church buddies" and their new friends once a quarter* just to connect,
affirm, encourage, and see where the gaps might be
that need to be addressed in assimilation and member
engagement strategies. This team then uses this information to plan next steps.

The prayerful intentionality of cultivating relationships among newcomers/guests and then among concentric circles of established members is critical for community building that does not end up as cliques. Learning to share your heart, preferences, struggles, successes, challenges, family connections, school and career connections, plus neighborhood connections builds bridges over time, sustains friendships, deepens investment in church, and works against creating cliques that isolate others.

Coachable churches move beyond business as usual. By claiming God's mission for all their church is and does, they look for meaning in every function—even meetings.

22

Ministering to Members on the Go

BALANCING GATHERED AND SCATTERED CHURCH MINISTRY

"COURAGE IS LIKE LOVE;
IT MUST HAVE HOPE FOR NOURISHMENT."
—Napoleon Bonaparte

I'm forever grateful for people who ministered to me. Ministry came in a variety of forms. I received countless cards, notes, and e-mail expressions of concern. People called and came by to visit with me. They listened and prayed for me. They fed me and provided many things I simply could not do alone to take care of my needs.

Church members often need ministry, as do people in the community. When a church begins to evaluate what is needed now to move the church forward, one area that's certain to be considered is ministry. We no longer live in an age when women of the church kept a freezer full of food, ready to take when crisis struck a member of the church or community. Crises today often seem to demand more than a home-cooked meal. What's a church to do to minister in the world today?

Churches have traditionally provided a variety of ministries. They provide funding for local and global ministries. They collect items—such as clothing, food, or household items—for people with needs. And they do hands-on ministry. We live in a world in which people prefer getting involved in hands-on ministry—serving on a local food truck to feed homeless people or going on a short-term mission trip.

Hands-on ministry is a disciple builder, even more than giving money or other items. One-on-one experiences with people in need develop stronger relationships with people being served, with fellow believers engaged in the ministry, and with God.

But people are busy! Crises generally aren't planned. Member needs like meals following the birth of a baby or surgery can be planned to some extent, but many needs take us by surprise. Churches may have become so inward focused that taking care of their own is the limit of their caregiving. Or they may be so involved in a variety of local ministries that now, with a smaller, aging membership, they can't keep up with their commitments. Finding balance can be a challenge!

Inward-focused churches have also tended to make ministry all about people in the churches. Members were expected to use their talents, gifts, and abilities to help the church function. Many members, active in organizations outside the church, were never recognized as being salt, light, and leaven on the Little League field, in the soup kitchen, or on the community center board. In addition to church-led and church-supported ministries, recognize and celebrate the good work your members are doing.

A few passages of Scripture are worth recalling at this point.

In Matthew 25, Jesus talked about judgment for people based on whether they helped those in need.

James wrote: "What good is it, my brothers and sisters, if you say you have faith but do not have works? Can faith save you? If a brother or sister is naked and lacks daily food, and one of you says to them, "Go in peace; keep warm and eat your fill," and yet you do not supply their bodily needs, what is the good of that? So faith by itself, if it has no works, is dead" (Jas. 2:14–17, NRSV).

We are called to care for others, and we are most fulfilled when we are doing what we are called to do!

Here are some practical ideas for on-the-go ministry designs:

- Establish culture and invite images that teach for all age groups and build a variety of delivery systems to share observations.
- Ordain/commission leaders to community recreational, social, health-care, or political environments as salt, light, and leaven in the world.

- Provide online connection, encouragement, and devotions for affinity groups.
- Provide online communities via social media, Skype, www.megameeting.com, Google plus, www.zoom.com, etc.
- Incorporate and value ministry of scattered church as much as gathered church reports in church services, budget, business meetings, etc.
- Create a missional metric for scattered church ministry experiences.
- What else?

COACHING QUESTIONS
1. Where in the world is the church? How would you answer this question?
2. Where is your church during the week?
3. How does your church encourage, equip, and support the church in the world each week?
4. How would you define your on-the-go members? Where are they going? What drives them there?

Five Things Your Church Leaders Can Do That Will Change Your Church in One Year
1. Seek to know and be obedient to the heart of God.
2. Prayerfully and authentically become friends with two unchurched persons.
3. Consistently engage those around you (churched or unchurched) in nonjudgmental dialogue about how, where, and when they experience God.
4. Bring your insights and struggles to your faith community as avenues of learning, stretching, and prayerful conversations.
5. Celebrate and share regularly the movement of God in and through your life and ministry.

PART V

Reflections on Reformation

Along with Martin Luther, I have beliefs and dreams about the future of the church, the reforms needed, and beliefs to be anchored in more relevant realities. As I consider church for the next fifty years, it seems...

- Church becomes more driven by authentic relationships than intellectualized doctrines.
- Church is less about place and more about people.
- Christianity's most respected expression will be from what is lived rather than proclaimed.
- Being church becomes more critical than attending church.
- Faith is nurtured in and through intentional reflection on life experiences.
- Creating redemptive structures and relationships becomes core for living as church.
- Aligning life with Christ's character, mission, and belief in others becomes key in marking maturity in faith and being church.
- Ministers lead through excellence in communication and collaboration, not so much through proclamation or visioning.
- Ministry financing comes through redemptive and missional networks and collaborative, passionate learners.
- Hope, healing, restoration, redemption, and reconciliation become key functions of a healthy church that impacts and influences all in various phases of spiritual formation.

- Grace and forgiveness become avenues of invitation and entry into wholeness and faith walk.
- Perfection is not the goal of believers; rather, a God-centered wholeness is.
- Leadership issues come from all who intentionally influence and impact the whole, the broken, and the restless.
- Prayer and discernment fuel empowered living and effective ministry as church in a wounded world.
- Mission of institution evolves into mission through life as experiences are connected to Divine truth.
- Membership in the church is replaced by functioning missionaries as the church.
- Spiritual formation becomes more about connecting to God, to others, and true-to-life experiences than connecting people to churches.
- Conversion is evidenced and worked on in all phases of life as connections to truth are discovered.
- The scattered church will become more visible and valued than the gathered church.

EPILOGUE

Why Believers Are Losing Interest in Church

Recovering Hope for Your Church begins with facing realities and moving beyond the comfort of denial, avoidance, and apathy. I have been deeply involved in church life and leadership all of my life! I believe in the church. I consider myself a mature Christian. I believe God ordained the church to join in the mission of God in the world. After living over a decade into the twenty-first century, I find I am deeply concerned about the church in North America! While some churches are growing and proving effective, many churches close their doors due to lack of funds, or participation, or both! Some researchers indicate that about 90–95 percent of existing North American churches are plateaued in attendance, and about 75 percent of the population is considered unchurched. Others predict we may lose about 60 percent of our existing churches in the next twenty years unless trends change now. Not only are the millennials leaving the church, but also a growing number of believers, church members, Christ followers are losing interest in an active participation in the institutional church. They are not giving up their faith, but rather see the institutional church as a barrier to living out their faith in our everchanging world. I have observed this in friends, colleagues, pastors, denominational leaders, family, and even in myself at times. I have a church leadership class that decided to be intentional about interviewing, spending time with, and engaging those believers losing interest in church. Over three months we mined our experiences through prayer, reflection, study, discussion, and uncovering our discoveries. The text below summarizes some of our findings through quotes we heard on more than a few occasions. We would love to hear your experiences and reflections too!

Below are the top 10 most-often-repeated quotes culled from over 200 interviews with persons who declared that, as believers, they are losing interest in church. It was really surprising to us, as we collected our data, how often almost these identical words were used in quotes from those unrelated persons we interviewed.

1. "Church adds little value to daily life experiences."
2. " We find it difficult to add value to and get involved in the church experience."
3. "Church is too inward focused in action, giving, and care!"
4. "Church talks about living by faith, but rarely takes risks into the new and unknown."
5. "Church has little interest and active involvement in justice issues of our day."
6. "Churches preach love, but practice hatred and judgment!"
7. "Churches are often dominated by a few people."
8. "Church rarely makes room for 'outsiders' in their leadership base."
9. "Pastors preach 'at us' rather than 'engaging us' in the scripture lesson."
10. "Churches typically use offerings for self-care rather than community engagement."

Granted, this qualitative research is only a beginning. The soft data has been gathered through interviews that have extended over time and, for many, created opportunities for ongoing dialogue and relationships. Many were so thrilled some church was really concerned about why so many believers were disinterested in church today. Most of those interviewed had, at one time, been faithful in attendance and active in leadership; they considered themselves believers. A few acknowledged they were "through with church." "Been there, done that!" was a familiar refrain, particularly from our "Busters" and "Gen X" sample.

What is the Spirit saying to you now? How does this article speak to you or your church?

The Reformation of the church continues through people like you and through churches like yours who exhibit great faith, courage, and resolve to be as effective as possible in the twenty-first–century world. Reflecting on lessons learned about *Recovering Hope for Your Church* and investing deeply in church and denominational life for more than thirty years of my life, I can honestly say I have more hope for the church than ever before in my life. Yes, many cultural and congregational issues could easily discourage a church leader, but I see many more evidences of God moving in the hearts and lives of people, businesses, and small groups of people inside and outside the church walls that give me great hope that God is up to something, and it's big! It is powerful, and it is fresh and new!

Movements such as Fresh Expressions, which started in England, have now shown up in many places around the world. Significant Bible study groups are bubbling up in workplaces across the globe. Nonprofits everywhere focus on niche groups to disciple and grow believers inside and outside the church walls. Certainly the traditional institutional models of church face challenges, but many churches will survive and even thrive as they respond to the Spirit of God in their midst and learn a new obedience of what it means to be faithful in a twenty-first–century world.

This book concludes a series of four books in the TCP Leadership Series in which I share my reflections of **A Church in Need of Conversion: Becoming Effective and Meaningful in a Twenty-First-Century World.**

Spiritual Leadership in a Secular Age: Building Bridges Instead of Barriers helped me frame the cultural shifts happening, and how they are impacting the way we do church today.

Reaching People under 40 While Keeping People over 60: Being Church for All Generations provides a practical philosophy of being church, fulfilling the call of Christ to speak to the distinctive needs of all age groups without isolating anyone.

Making Shifts without Making Waves is the how-to guidebook for leaders trying to implement the concepts of *Reaching People under 40 While Keeping People over 60.* We introduce the coach approach leadership style that is needed to make the concepts a reality and contextualized to a variety of ministry contexts.

Recovering Hope for Your Church: Moving beyond Maintenance and Missional to Incarnational Engagement is a personal and corporate journey that provides practical tools and strategies for moving forward to deepen the impact of church. The journey of recovering hope may be tough for many, but it is well worth it!

The journey into and out of recovery brought deep transformation to me. I have realized a diseased, infected, tired, lifeless body often experiences frustration, aimlessness, apathy, and atrophy. Rebuilding the physical body or the body of Christ (the church) calls for reform, rehabilitation, and renewal for recovery to happen. I have no doubt that leadership and structure must change for the institutional church to stay relevant in our current age. The

God of Scripture does not change, but the ways God comes to and moves people have found fresh expressions throughout church history, and we are experiencing the move again. This reality frightens some, and for others it brings great hope and calm that God is with us—even now.

May your reading and practice of these concepts in your life, your small group, your faith community, church, or denomination bring great hope, satisfaction, and knowing that God is with you, that God is still moving people to a deeper faith to impact the world in ways that bring pleasure to our Creator and fulfillment to those of us who choose to follow God to places unknown. The concepts here are certain to stretch you beyond your comfort zones, deepen your faith, and call you to experience the heights and depths of the love of God in ways you or your church have never known. Go forth and be the church in a world that needs the presence of grace, hope, healing, health, and assurance that God is with us!

APPENDICES

Toolkit for
Recovering Hope for
Your Church

COACHNG TOOLS

- Cultural Impact on Church Practices
- I Dream of a Church…
- What Drives Your Leadership?
- Missional Measurements
- Innovative Models of Christian Education
- Where Will Your Church Be in Five to Ten Years?

Additional coaching tools and how to use them effectively are part of the "Congregational Coach Certification," designed and delivered by Edward Hammett and The Columbia Partnership and Cooperative Baptist Fellowship of North Carolina. For details, go to www. TransformingSolutions.org, www.TheColumbiaPartnership.org, or www.cbfnc.org.

Cultural Impact on Church Practices
(What and How Cultural Shifts Impact Church Practices)

CHURCH CULTURE PRACTICES (1940s–1970s)	POST-CHURCH CULTURE PRACTICES (1960s–2014+)
Primary meetings on Sunday/Wednesday	Multiple services at most convenient time/place
Centralized worship, education, church	Decentralized worship, discipleship, church
Increased number of programs for all age groups	Streamlining programming around functions for intergenerational grouping
Family-focused language and ministries (biologically connected)	Family being redefined, calling for new language, options
Pastor-centered pastoral care and church management	Lay-led pastoral care and missional leadership and practices
Success defined by managing and tracking numbers of visits, budget, attendance, etc.	Success defined by measuring impact, influence of lay leaders in the work-a-day world
Budgets, programming designed to meet needs of attending congregational members	Budgets, programming designed as missional strategies for those inside and outside church walls
Churchwide visitation nights	Connection happens through technology, scheduled visits with purpose and meaning
Centralized curricula design and publication	Decentralized, contextualized curricula design and publication
Male-dominated church and denominational leadership	Increasing role of women in church and denominational leadership
Anglo domination	Multicultural, multiethnic emergence
Building-housed church and maintenance is focused on values, vision, and funding	Church building no longer the place of church values, vision, or funding for maintenance
Staffing designed around age groups' needs and desires	Staffing is increasingly home-grown; part-time and/or multicareer rather than full-time
Seminary-trained, program-driven leadership models	Mentor-driven and proven contextualized programming and leadership models
Pastoral relationship committee or deacons managing pastor/staff duties and accountability	Pastor/staff supervision is done by 360 degree supervision by one another and those they work with in programming
Committee-driven management	Collaborative, short-term, project-focused teams engaged in missional and incarnational ministries

Pastor-led worship—verbal sermons, traditional music	Worship planned by lay/clergy worship teams, visual-driven sermons, contextualized music often primarily lay-led and lay-driven
Denominational loyalties dominate decision making	Congregational groupings become primary avenue for collaborative learning, giving, going
Tithes/offerings of membership primary way of funding ministries	Creating and sustaining multiple streams of income and engaging in e-giving options become core of creative funding of ministries
Focused on giving to missionaries and mission causes around the world	Focused on creating missionaries of members that are active in global missions at home and beyond homeland

I dream of a church...

❑ that invests more in people than property; that generates ministries from giftedness and call of people rather than the generic versions from the past.

❑ that mobilizes lay ministers in God's mission in the world and not just ministering inside the church walls...

❑ that clings more to God than to familiar traditions.

❑ whose pastors are more passionate and committed to equipping the saints for the work of the ministry than just committed to keeping the saints happy.

❑ that begins each team/committee meeting with, "What is God doing in our church and community?" rather than, "What is the pastor doing and how's the budget doing?" Refocusing on mission, not maintenance, moves churches forward. Focusing on maintenance issues of budgets and buildings and personnel keeps churches stuck!

❑ that is organized for mobilizing, community experiences, missional focus, and disciplemaking strategies instead of being organized around traditions, age groups, or traditional program designs.

❑ that points people to the love and service of God rather than to a church's history or personal preferences.

❑ that nurtures community amidst diversity rather than nurturing elitism.

❑ that develops giftedness and callings instead of greed and comfort.

❑ that is driven by, "Let's try it," rather than "We've never done it that way before."
❑ that takes risks to nurture faith, rather than preserving comfort zones that nurture contentment and complacency.

"My dreams make me who I am"...
What do your dreams make you?

Today, a church's greatest challenge is to connect with those God calls them to reach. The church's greatest fear is moving from their familiar routines to reach the unreached. The church's greatest obligation is to be pleasing to God. The church's greatest hope is found in mobilizing those in the pew rather than just changing those in the pulpit.

What Drives Your Leadership?
(Self-Assessment Reflection)

INSTRUCTIONS: Prayerfully reflect on your leadership function for the last year as you review the following columns describing two different types of leadership. Put an asterisk (*) beside each of those that describe what drives your decisions and actions as a leader in your church.

COACHING QUESTIONS TO CONSIDER

1. What does your response say to you?
2. How would you label/describe each column of leadership styles?
3. If you were to put a percent that accurately reflects your preferred style, use of resources, etc., as a leader, what would it be?
4. Now place a checkmark beside each characteristic you feel would improve the impact and effectiveness of your leadership if you embraced the focus.
5. What are two things you will do to integrate your challenge into your leadership in the coming months?
6. Who can help you with this?
7. Whom can you learn from?

Typically focused on nurture of the membership, ill, and homebound	Focused on creating redemptive, healing, justice relationships and partnership
Inward focused	Outward focused
Success measured by visits, contacts, prayers, presence	Success measured by advocacy, healing, redemptive opportunities engaged in over time
Motive: to satisfy needs, desires of congregation	Motive: to satisfy needs, desires of God
Typically congregational focused	Ultimately world/community focused
Calls for time, presence, votes, follow-through, prayer	Calls for faith, risk-taking, discernment, consensus, engagement, discomfort
Maintenance focus/gathered church	Missional and incarnational focus/scattered church
Private, confidential, people driven	Collaborative, celebrative, challenge driven
Focus is nurture, caregiving of those we know	Focus is on those we need to know and care for through advocacy, concern, engagement
Focuses on those in crisis and those who call for and expect care as we do church	Stretches us to be church for those who often have no voice but need our voice and presence
Emerges from voiced needs/expectations	Emerges from sitting in solitude/prayer, listening, and "observing all things"; paying attention to the holy nudgings
Manage people and need requests	Willing to live in messiness of missional engagement where you seek next steps and focus on alignment more than management
Resources are people, time, money from congregation	Resources are from inside and outside the community of faith
Keeps the institution in place and happy	Moves church into the world as the body of Christ

Missional Measurements
(Learning to Measure What Matters as a Missional Church)

PURPOSE OF EVALUATION TOOL

1. Clarifies what drives behavior and beliefs
2. Clarifies focus, intentionality in ministry
3. Provides assessment tools for leaders and churches

CONSIDER

1. Number of church members volunteering in local community positions _____
2. Number of church members serving as volunteers in local church positions _____
3. Number of hours members volunteer in the community _____
4. Number of hours members volunteer in the church _____
5. Percentage of church budget spent on members _____
6. Percentage of church budget spent on personnel _____
7. Percentage of church budget spent on nonchurch members _____
8. Percentage of church budget spent on outreach _____
9. Percentage of meeting agendas given to membership needs _____
10. Percentage of meeting agendas given to community needs _____
11. Percentage of ministry programming designed with membership needs in mind _____
12. Percentage of ministry programming designed with nonchurch members in mind _____
13. Percentage of prayer focus of members on membership or persons related to membership circle of relatives/friends _____
14. Percentage of prayer time given to persons beyond church members or their family/friends _____
15. Percentage of facilities designed with members' needs in mind _____
16. Percentage of facilities designed with nonmembers' needs in mind _____
17. Other _____

Instructions: Using the provided continuum, self-assess your real response rather than desired response or behavior to each issue above. Where on the continuum would you place your previous responses to each question?

<---|--->

Maintenance   **Missional**   **Incarnational**

• What are your insights/learnings from this exercise?

• What would make each response more missional and incarnational in your church?

• What are the likely barriers to this happening in your context?

• How can these barriers be addressed?

• Who can help you move forward?

• What is a reasonable timeline and next step for you now?

Innovative Models of Christian Education*

FRESH EXPRESSIONS

- www.freshexpressionsusa.org

THE WAY MAKERS

- www.waymakers.org

DECENTRALIZED

- www.bibleseries.com
- Animate: Bible – Brian McLaren www.wearesparkhouse.org

INTERGENERATIONAL

- www.LifeLongFaith.com
- http://www.lifelongfaith.com/uploads/5/1/6/4/5164069/becoming_intentionally_intergenerational_-_roberto.pdf

SOMA COMMUNITIES

- Living out mission as the church in the cities
- www.somacommunities.org

DIGITIZED LEARNING AS YOU GO

- www.waymakers.org
- Seeking God for the Cities: Steve Hawthorne, 800-264-5214

APPS FOR CHRISTIAN EDUCATION

- Assembly of God: www.714movement.org
- Clips-app.com
- Movie clips: www.wingclips.com
- Logos Bible App
- Church on the Go / Leadership Training on the Go
- www.TransformingSolutions.org
- www.bibleseries.tv
- Generosity Issues for Next-Generation Churches http://lead net.org/resources/download/generousity_becoming_a_fundamental_spritual_discipline_for_churches
- Designed to facilitate spiritual formation and Christian growth www.spiritfireapp.com

CHILDREN'S MINISTRY

- Children and Family Ministry: www.seattlequest.org

YOUTH MINISTRY

- www.unfilteredMagazine.com
- www.collegeministrythoughts.com
- www.ymtcchstuff.com
- Live curriculum: www.live.simplyyouthministry.com
- Ministry and Media by Scott Firestone IV Group Magazine www.groupmagazine.com
- The Simple Truth Bible–downloadable daily devotions
- www.simplyyouthministry.com

MISSION TRIP SPIRITUAL FORMATION FOR FAMILIES

- www.21stcenturyfaithformation.org

CHURCH AT WORK MINISTRIES

- Doug Spada: www.worklife.org
- David Miller: www.avodahinstitute.com
- John Bost: www.churchforeclosure.org

GIFT DISCOVERY BY CHRISTIAN SWARTZ

- http://3colorworld.org/en/surveys/ministry/summary/ about

* This listing is not meant to be exhaustive, but rather indicative of some of the fresh work emerging as God is about, doing new things in our twenty-first-century world.

Where Will the Church Be in Five to Ten Years?
(Trends to Watch and Consider in Planning)

TRENDS TO WATCH	POSSIBLE RESPONSES INCLUDE ...			
	SPIRITUAL FORMATION	ORGANIZA- TIONAL	FUNDING/ RESOURCING	STAFFING/ LEADERSHIP
Diversity of Community and Church Population				
Generational Shifts - Learning Styles - Worship Styles - Other				
Decreasing Denomination- alism and Loyalty				
Changing Family Structures - Multicultural - Single Parents - Nonbiological - Dual Careers - Other				
Decentralizing of Church - Structures - Curricula				
Regional Design of Curricula - Multiple Delivery Systems				
Reframing of Church Functions/ Purpose for Increasingly Secular Population - Finding Christ in a Secular Culture				
New Leadership Structures/Staffing Emerging Due to Generational Issues, Economy, and Diversity				
Increasing Impact of Technology on Spiritual Development of All Ages				

Funding of Ministry beyond the Tithe - Missional-Based Entrepreneurs Emerge				
Partnerships, Collaboration, and Congregational Coaching; Coaches Become the New "Normal" for Core Values of Growing Ministries				

COACHING QUESTIONS

1. What else?
2. What questions does this surface?
3. How can you move forward and be proactive rather than reactive?

NOTES

Preface: The Power of Why

1. Henry Cloud, *Necessary Endings: The Employees, Businesses, and Relationships That All of Us Have to Give Up in Order to Move Forward* (New York: Harper, 2011), 15–16.

2. Findley B. Edge, *A Quest for Vitality in Religion* (Nashville: Broadman, 1963), 1.

3. Ibid., 21–22.

Chapter 3: Uncovering Blind Spots and Lies Leaders Perpetuate

1. Mike Regele with Mark Schulz, *Death of the Church* (Grand Rapids, Mich.: Zondervan, 1995).

2. Findley B. Edge, *A Quest for Vitality in Religion* (Nashville: Broadman, 1963).

Chapter 4: Scope of Transitions Facing Churches–Tying History to Hope

1. G. Jeffrey MacDonald, "Who's in the Pews?" *The Christian Science Monitor Weekly* (December 24, 2012): 27–29.

Chapter 9: Bullying in the Church and What to Do about It

1. I address this in detail in Edward Hammett and James Pierce, *Reaching People under 40 While Keeping People over 60* (Saint Louis: Chalice Press, 2007).

2. Gordon MacDonald, *Who Stole My Church? What to Do When the Church You Love Tries to Enter the Twenty-first Century* (Nashville: Thomas Nelson, 2007).

3. Alan Deutschman, *Change or Die: The Three Keys to Change at Work and in Life* (New York: HarperBusiness, 2007).

4. Ibid.

5. Edward Hammett and James Pierce, *Making Shifts without Making Waves: A Coach Approach to Soulful Leadership* (Saint Louis: Chalice Press, 2007).

Chapter 11: The Power of Congregational Coaching

1. Coach training and coaches are available to help you. I have designed a Congregational Coach Certification program that provides training, toolkits for coaches, and a more detailed treatment of this template. For details, go to www.TransformingSolutions.org, www.CBFNC.org, www.ca-ministries.com, or www.TheColumbiaPartnership.org.

Chapter 17: Signs of and Solutions for an Overprogrammed Church

1. Eddy Hall, adapted by Eddie Hammett from *Leadership Journal*, Fall 1999, 111.

2. For additional information about new staffing models, explore Edward Hammett, *Spiritual Leadership in a Secular Age* (Saint Louis: Chalice Press, 2005).

3. Contact www.transformingsolutions.org or www.thecolumbiapartnership.org for coaching services.

Chapter 18: Rebooting Your Church–When? How?

1. Jen Hatmaker, *7: An Experimental Mutiny against Excess* (Nashville: B&H Publishing Group, 2012).

Chapter 20: Making Events More Meaningful Experiences of Transformation

1. Patrick Lencioni, *Death by Meeting: A Leadership Fable about Solving the Most Painful Problem in Business* (New York: Jossey-Bass, 2004).

2. Chad Hall and Linda Miller, *Christian Coaching for Leaders: A Practical Guide* (Saint Louis: Chalice Press, 2007); Jane Creswell, *The Complete Idiot's Guide to Coaching for Excellence* (New York: Alpha, 2008).

About the Author

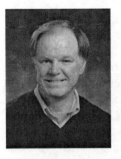

Eddie has served on church staff and in denominational leadership for over twenty-five years. He is a prolific author, Professional Certified Coach (PCC) with the International Coach Federation, popular speaker, and a retreat and seminar leader across the country. He has worked among more than twelve denominations and judicatories. Eddie is President of Transforming Solutions, a founding coach of Valwood Christian Leadership Coaching (www.valwoodcoaching.com), a coach with The Columbia Partnership (www.thecolumbiapartnership.org), and an affiliate with Coach Approach Ministries (www.ca-ministries.com). He currently serves in a partnership with Cooperative Baptist Fellowship of North Carolina www.cbfnc.org as their Church and Clergy Coach. His coaching experiences are deep and wide, touching churches of various denominations, church planters, and lay and clergy leaders across the country.

Eddie is the author of seven books dealing with preparing the church for a more effective ministry in the twenty-first century. He has also authored over 400 published articles. Leonard Sweet invited Eddie to contribute coaching questions to *The Gospel According to Starbucks* released in 2007. His most recent best-selling book is *Reaching People under 40 while Keeping People over 60,* Chalice press, 2007. The companion piece to the Reaching/Keeping book is *Making Shifts Without Making Waves: A Coach Approach to Soulful Leadership,* released October, 2009.

Recovering Hope for Your Church is the fourth book in Eddie's leadership series designed to help leaders, congregations, and denominations improve effectiveness of ministry in a twenty-first–century culture. Eddie has also served as a lead coach for the Sustaining Pastoral Excellence project funded by the Lilly Foundation to develop coaching strategies for pastors and congregations across the Southeast United States and across denominational lines. On his personal website www.transformingsolutions.org you will find free leadership newsletters to assist in the coach approach to church, non-profit organizational development, programming, and local church and denominational ministries.

Persons like Bill Easum, Tom Bandy, and Leonard Sweet invite Eddie to lead online and face-to-face national seminars on themes related to his published writings. His seminars, coaching, and leadership cross denominational lines as he has worked with American Baptists, Presbyterians, United Methodists, Free Will Baptists, Lutherans, The Church of Our Lord Jesus Christ of the Apostolic Age, Southern Baptists, and Cooperative Baptist Fellowship. He has enjoyed being the plenary speaker in 2013-2014 for Southeast Jurisdiction Cabinet Consultation for UMC and the Academy of Leadership Excellence.

Eddie's call to ministry is to "equip the saints for the work of ministry" inside and beyond the walls of the traditional church. He lives out this calling through his consulting, coaching, and writing ministry and through his personal ministry serving as a life coach for a growing number of "spiritual travelers" (persons on a serious spiritual journey, but not connected consistently to a traditional church).

Eddie has been mentored and coached through the years by many who have deeply influenced his life and ministry. Dr. Findley Edge was his mentor during and beyond seminary days. L.D. Johnson, William Clemmons, Gordon and Mary Cosby, Ken Smith, Reid Hardin, George Bullard, Jane Creswell, MCC; Linda Miller, MCC; Suzanne Goebel, PCC; and countless others have influenced his life and ministry.

He is a graduate of Furman University, Southern Baptist Theological Seminary with postgraduate studies at Duke Divinity School, Southeastern Seminary, NC State University, and Fielding Institute. He has lectured at or served as adjunct faculty at Gardner-Webb Divinity School, Northern Baptist Seminary, Southeastern Baptist Seminary, Duke Divinity School, Western Seminary, Golden Gate Seminary, Southern Seminary and Campbell Divinity School.